THE
SALES
MBA

THE
SALES
MBA

How to Influence Corporate Buyers

Douglas Cole

BARLOW BOOKS
fine books for enterprising authors

Library and Archives Canada Cataloguing in Publication data available upon request.

978-1-988025-85-8 (paperback)

Printed in Canada

Publisher: Sarah Scott
Book producer: Tracy Bordian/At Large Editorial Services
Cover design: Alison Garnett
Interior design and layout: Ruth Dwight
Copy editing: Joel Gladstone
Indexing: Wendy Thomas

For more information, visit **www.barlowbooks.com**

Barlow Book Publishing Inc.
96 Elm Avenue, Toronto, ON
Canada M4W 1P2

For Dr. Sholto Fletcher Cole
(1931–2020)

Contents

THE MINDSET ADVANTAGE

Anyone who has worked in sales will recall a moment of soul-crushing humiliation. One of my own memories remains painfully clear. I had finally managed to connect with a senior executive after several failed attempts. She was caught off guard, and she made it clear that I had reached her not because of the effectiveness of my outreach but because her standard defense system had somehow failed to detect my breach. Nevertheless, now that I had her on the phone, she reluctantly signaled that she would hear me out, at least for a moment. However, after just a couple of sentences, I could already sense the conversation was going nowhere. She immediately went on the offensive, speaking over me and aggressively repeating her question until I was forced to answer it. "Are you trying to sell me something?" she demanded to know. I was blinded with rage, incensed that someone could be so rude when I had shown her nothing but respect. I gave an equivocal response, claiming that the question couldn't be answered until we both had a better sense of what she and her team needed. She promptly hung up the phone, and I stared into the distance as I contemplated her evil nature, my fantasy resignation, and the general futility of the human project.

This exchange highlights the deep divide that every sales professional is forced to cross. Jerry Seinfeld once observed that "sales help" is an oxymoron: "You're either helping me or selling me, but they're not the same thing." There is pervasive resistance, if not outright hostility, to a seller's agenda. Becoming a "trusted advisor" seems impossible when the truth is that salespeople are not, strictly speaking, disinterested. They have an undeniable commercial agenda. If we acknowledge this agenda, then it appears we must also accept that sellers are never "objective" in the true sense of the term.

And yet, after watching hundreds of salespeople evolve from bungling to best-in-class, I've seen a fascinating phenomenon play out repeatedly. What I've seen is a gradual progression in mindset for those who master the craft:

- *Stage 1—Likeability:* When people start out in sales, they tend to be emotionally conflicted. On some level they are uncomfortable about the fact that their job is to get a stranger—typically, a very busy stranger—to buy something that they may not actually need. The seller manages this discomfort by trying to be as likeable and charming as possible.

- *Stage 2—Mutuality:* At some point sellers embrace their material self-interest. They overcome their shyness about having a commercial agenda because they feel it can be counterbalanced with an equal emphasis on benefits to the client. They start to use the language of "win-win" outcomes, indicating that they have arrived at the level of mutuality.

- *Stage 3—Objectivity:* Only a small percentage of sellers achieve what I would call plausible objectivity. This level is not a repudiation of the previous two stages. On the contrary, top-tier sellers have terrific relationships and they are adept at creating mutually beneficial outcomes. But these are the fruits of trust and the natural consequence of a more detached view of the factors that influence a sale. From the client's perspective, a plausibly objective seller is the most valuable seller one can work with. From the seller's perspective, it's also the most difficult mental state to achieve.

The goal of this book is to help you achieve this mental state more quickly. In a moment I'll explain my teaching framework, but first I should acknowledge what you are probably thinking. I suspect there's a traffic cop standing at the crosswalk of your attention, and that you're waiting for a signal on whether to pause, proceed, or pivot in a new direction. You're waiting, in other words, for an answer to the obvious question: *Is this book for me?* That's the question any honest and respectful author must directly address.

The Sales MBA is written for you if you want to get better at influencing corporate buyers. You could be a sales professional who works with "enterprise" clients. You could be a start-up founder who sells business-to-business (B2B) products or services. Or you could be a direct influencer who allocates money and people within your company. If you are an enterprise sales professional, I consider you to be the primary audience. However, if you find that "selling" your idea to corporate stakeholders is an increasingly vital part of what you do—as is the case for many people in today's economy—then this book will also help.

I'm calling out these readers because they are best represented among the hundreds of people with whom I've tested and refined this material. The journey to *The Sales MBA* began with a "Mini-MBA for Sales" program I developed as a side project for LinkedIn's global sales organization. Many LinkedIn employees—not only those without a formal business education but also those who were interested in a refresher—told me how much they benefitted from the principles and tactics we'll cover.

That feedback prompted me to take the curriculum to an external audience with comparable interests, so I began testing some of the concepts in my part-time mentoring role with start-up accelerators in Canada and the US. The founders I work with are bright, energetic, and highly motivated to evangelize their product or service with corporate buyers, but they typically lack experience in sales. I repackaged the Mini-MBA as a three-part series to give these founders a crash course in the theory and practices of effective B2B selling. Feedback from hundreds of them confirmed the high value of the course.

Finally, in my capacity as a part-time lecturer at the Rotman School of Management, University of Toronto, I have used much of this material in a Consulting Fundamentals class for second-year MBA students. These students are looking to become trusted advisors to large corporations. They learn the theoretical foundations of consulting, and my colleagues and I coach them through pro bono engagements with large institutional clients. Informally and through course feedback, they've helped me validate what works best in getting executives to stand behind ambitious change proposals.

While sales professionals are more narrowly focused on selling than start-up founders and knowledge workers, I believe selling skills are an important, and frequently overlooked, competency in general. The skill of selling is only becoming more critical as the competition for people's attention gets increasingly fierce—and with no end in sight. Your product, your service, and your idea have never had to contend with such a formidable array of compelling alternatives. Back in 2012, Dan Pink observed that persuading and influencing was taking up at least 40 percent of knowledge workers' time.[1] That number is almost certainly higher today. And yet, across almost 5,000 colleges and universities in the US, fewer than 200 have courses or programs in sales.[2] The craft of selling remains largely self-taught, despite being an indispensable skill for any well-rounded knowledge worker.

There are understandable reasons for this. For one thing, it's difficult to generalize about what works in sales. Context is paramount, and former superstars will often turn out to be disappointing in a different industry, company, or team. In addition, selling is something that is apparently best learned by doing. Consider well-known entrepreneurs who are universally esteemed for their sales acumen: Sara Blakley, Daymond John, or Howard Schultz, for example. All of them spent considerable time in the trenches, hawking shoes (Blakley), clothes (John), and Xerox products (Schultz) to hone their formidable talents.

Despite, or perhaps because of, the lack of formal sales programs in post-secondary education, the market for sales training is immense. This explains the apparently endless supply of how-to materials on offer. Thousands of books, consultants, and online instructors claim they can, in fact, teach you how to sell. I've gone through many of these materials, and they've taught me a lot. But I've also noticed they lack something, especially when it comes to the challenge of engaging corporate buyers.

To understand the missing element, it helps to remember that there are generally three ways to teach adult learners. Imagine you are instructing a group of knowledge workers on how to be more productive. You could show them tools and hacks to squeeze more hours from the day. You could explain how to run meetings, organize their calendars, or take effective notes. Or you could encourage them to take a step back and rethink their approach to time management in general. You could argue, as Oliver Burkeman has, that productivity is a trap, and that the real measure of any time management system is whether it helps you neglect the right things. In other words, you could take either a tool-set, skill-set, or mindset approach.

Most of the instructional materials you find in any industry will focus on skills and tools because these are the easiest things to teach, and that's what I've noticed in sales literature as well. Think about it. What will get a novice from 0 to 90 percent mastery most efficiently and effectively? Tactics and techniques will deliver the greatest ROI every time. You start out in a new sport, for example, by learning the rules, buying the right gear, and refining your coordination. That's what gets you to a point of high competence. But going from 90 to 100 requires a different approach. At that point it's no longer simply about the shoes you wear or the movements you make. It's about the attitude you bring to every practice and game. It becomes more about mindset.

Mindset is what I'm going to emphasize in *The Sales MBA*, and it's what sets this book apart from the rest of B2B sales literature today. I won't ignore the skills dimension at all. In fact, I'll share many examples of what top-performing sellers do in the line of fire, so to speak. But these tactical examples are nested in a new framework for B2B sales. I'm encouraging sales professionals to see themselves differently, to embrace a more elevated view of what they do on the job. I'm recommending you step back and take stock of the full field. I believe this new perspective will help you achieve plausible objectivity with your clients and stakeholders. It will also make you a more effective influencer.

To get us there, I believe we need to revisit the first principles of sales. When I reference "first principles," I'm talking about the basic building blocks of knowledge. Blogger Tim Urban once contrasted cooks and chefs to illustrate a first-principles approach. He explained that chefs work from first principles because they understand how raw ingredients combine to create an infinite array of flavor possibilities. Cooks, by contrast, follow a recipe. While both chefs and cooks can create a delicious meal, only chefs understand why the food tastes good. Cooks are unconsciously competent in the kitchen. They essentially mimic what others have already done. They prefer to operate on autopilot, and they tend to be stymied by the unexpected. Chefs have a deeper understanding of what works. They can imagine a wider range of options, and they can quickly adjust to missing elements as they prepare a meal.

The Sales MBA focuses on the first principles of sales to maximize your creative freedom. From what I've observed, the best B2B sales professionals view a sales conversation through three overlapping filters. First, they examine the external environment, and they learn how their client's company is positioned within it. That means figuring out who the key competitors are and what the client must to do defend or improve its market-facing position. Second, they look at the organizational context, and they identify the internal sources of energy. That means identifying the dominant themes and most influential players at any given time. Third, they look at the interpersonal dimension, determining what's needed to engage individual buyers and influencers. That means tailoring their message to ensure it is not only understood but acted upon. These are what I consider the "raw ingredients" of enterprise selling, and they define the core framework of this book. Here's a quick overview of what lies ahead.

PART I: BECOMING A STRATEGIST

Effective sellers understand business fundamentals. They know what it takes for a company to succeed in a competitive industry. They explicitly connect the value of their product or service to a company's clearest path to victory. This is what it takes to be considered a Strategist. In plain and direct language, I'll explain what a business strategy is, and how sellers can use this knowledge to build trust and credibility with executive buyers.

PART II: BECOMING A CHANGE AGENT

Effective sellers know how to navigate complex organizational dynamics. They recognize that people and companies are typically resistant to change. They understand the variables that slowly reshape people's motivation and ability. They are adept at working with these variables to guide the transformation of the client organization. I'll break down a best-in-class framework to help structure your efforts as a Change Agent.

PART III: BECOMING A DECISION ARCHITECT

Effective sellers are sophisticated psychologists. They are fascinated by the quirks of human nature, including the wide variety of subconscious influences that sway our personal and professional decisions. They seek to understand the deeper drivers of human behavior, and they use this knowledge to inform their communications and sales approach. I'll walk you through six important principles from behavioral economics that have practical implications for the seller as a Decision Architect.

PART IV: WIDENING OUR LENS

In the last section I'll zoom out and tie the above concepts together. First, I'll discuss why the world of B2B sales is evolving in a way that demands a new breed of sales professional, one that incorporates the core themes of this book. Second, I'll describe the broader implications of integrating Strategist, Change Agent, and Decision Architect principles into your life and work.

As I've said, the primary audience for *The Sales MBA* are B2B sales professionals. Despite that ostensibly specialist focus, however, I believe this book has generalist applications, much as bodybuilding or ballet techniques can be useful to those who wish to improve their strength and flexibility but have no intention of becoming the next Arnold Schwarzenegger or Anna Pavlova. The principles and tactics we cover will be helpful to you as you grapple with influence challenges, even if you don't carry a sales quota.

This book is framed as a "Sales MBA" because, like a business school program, it's meant to build a common understanding of frameworks and approaches that help to address company challenges. But I'm also suggesting there's a mismatch between a traditional MBA curriculum and the practice of sales. Selling skills are not substantially improved with a better understanding of accounting, finance, or marketing. As someone who holds an MBA and has transitioned from consulting to sales, I can firmly attest to this. However, business acumen is indeed a powerful lever in sales, and it remains a growth area for many sales professionals. But we should specify what we mean by "business acumen." For selling to corporate buyers, I believe it amounts to understanding how companies make money, how organizations evolve, and how people make decisions. Those are the ground realities of B2B selling, and they are the organizing principles of this book.

Years ago, when I was onboarded at LinkedIn, I recall being inspired by the company's stated intention to "elevate the sales profession." I see this book as an extension of that vision. I've come to regard Strategist, Change Agent, and Decision Architect skills as elements of the mindset required to establish oneself as a trusted advisor. I hope to sharpen your perception of the forces that shape buying decisions so you can work with them more deliberately. I also hope to dignify the discipline of sales, helping those who influence and sell find greater focus and fulfillment in their work.

PART I: BECOMING A STRATEGIST

"It's not how well you play the game. It's deciding what game you want to play."

—KWAME APPIAH

CHAPTER 1

Where Do They Compete?
How Will They Win?

I remember one of the most valuable lessons I learned from a senior leader at LinkedIn. He was advising a sales team on how to communicate to executives. He gave it to them straight, explaining how executives tend to process information throughout the day. For context, he reminded the audience what a typical executive's schedule feels like. He explained that executives move from one meeting to the next, switching focus at an unforgiving pace. Naturally, to preserve their mental energy, they come to rely on filters. In transitioning to each new meeting, they tend to ask themselves two simple questions: *Does this matter?* and *How's it going?* In other words, they first want to determine whether the topic is worth paying attention to. If it is, they also want to know what needs to be done. In essence, these two questions, and the practice of continually asking them, explain what gets people promoted to an executive role in the first place. The questions reveal an instinct for focusing on company value and habitually solving problems.

This is a crucial insight as we begin the discussion of how to sell to corporate buyers. If you're selling to an enterprise client, chances are that an executive will ultimately make or approve the buying decision. Consider that in your first contact with this executive you'll generally have about 60 seconds in which to capture their attention. That means you'll need a frame to quickly communicate the value of your initiative (*Does this matter?*). Strategy is such a frame. Strategy is the primary basis for corporate investments. Strategy determines the allocation of limited resources, whether we're talking about money or people. Strategy is the language of the executive ranks within a firm, and you as a seller need to be at least conversant in this language.

The challenge is that "strategy" has become a nebulous term. In hundreds of coaching conversations with salespeople, I've often posed the following question: "What's the strategy of your most important client?" The question usually triggers a confused expression or a halting attempt to stitch together a patchwork of observations. Rarely has anyone answered it crisply and with confidence. Think about that. It is the cardinal responsibility of a sales professional to understand their client's business. In the case of a seller's "most important" client, you'd think this responsibility would be greater still.

To be sure, sales reps are not the only ones who struggle with the term. The truth is that, for many of us, strategy is not such an easy thing to define. It feels incredibly difficult to whittle something as complex as a company strategy down to a few sentences. This is partly because we've diluted and distorted the meaning of "strategy" over the years. The word is now used so promiscuously and imprecisely that people no longer understand its conceptual parameters. To give a random example, I remember a meeting in which a senior leader circulated a slide deck as a pre-read, the purpose of which was to "discuss our strategy for the year." In essence, it said that we planned to grow by a certain percentage, and then it broke that growth target down across each of our main lines of business. During the meeting I asked for more details beyond the financial objectives outlined in the deck, but it soon became clear such details hadn't been fleshed out.

These situations are commonplace. They show how our conventional interpretation of strategy has become analogous to what former US Supreme Court Justice Potter Stewart once said was his threshold for determining whether something met the definition of "obscenity" ("I know it when I see it"). In other words, "strategy" has become purely subjective and sorely lacking in definitional boundaries.

I believe this represents an important opportunity for you as a seller. Consider the basic facts again: Strategy is the most powerful frame for executive decisions, and yet strategic conversations often seem like tennis matches being played with hockey sticks. You'll have a significant advantage as a seller if you show up with the proper equipment. You'll be able to draw a clear line between your product or service and what is in your client's best interest. While other sellers may present themselves in vague and self-seeking terms, you'll be direct and focused. You'll stand out as someone who can definitively answer the question, "Does this matter?"

The rest of this section is devoted to reclaiming the value and utility of a clear understanding of "strategy," so that you can better position yourself with corporate buyers. As a first step, let's be clear about what strategy is *not*. In Table 1.1 below, the five statements in the left-hand column masquerade as strategies, when in fact the labels on the right are a more accurate description.

Table 1.1

"STRATEGY"	TRANSLATION
"To achieve top-quartile recognition."	Performance Goal
"To surpass $10 billion in revenue."	Financial Target
"To create a better everyday life for the many people."	Vision Statement
"We appreciate that all life on earth is under threat of extinction. We aim to use the resources we have—our business, our investments, our voice and our imaginations—to do something about it."	Mission Statement
"To crush our quota."	Hope

I have a theory as to why these have all become widely accepted substitutes for strategy. I believe it's because, in thinking about the purpose of a business, many of us see a spectrum that runs from the conceptual to the specific, and we feel the need to take a side. It's difficult to stand squarely in the middle of that spectrum, and to find words to define such a position. By default, we gravitate to one end or the other. Those who are inclined to abstract thinking use the language of vision and mission. Those who favor tangible facts and figures focus on goals and targets. Our default is the manifestation of differences in temperament. However, as we'll discuss in a moment, strategy is a term that straddles these two extremes. It's a concept that integrates the general and the particular. For this reason, the term is not intuitive for most of us. It requires effort to slow down and distill its key elements.

I've spent a lot of time going through the literature in search of a simple and practical construct, and it's easy to get lost in the library. (For fellow bookworms, I've included an extensive reading list at the end of this book.) However, I would say a few resources stand out. Sir Lawrence Freedman's *Strategy: A History* is an interesting survey of the evolution of military, political, and business strategy. But, in the end, it accepts the slipperiness of the term by conceding that "there is no agreed-upon definition of strategy that describes the field and limits its boundaries."[3]

Three books stand in opposition to Freedman's perspective: Roger Martin's *Playing to Win*, Richard Rumelt's *Good Strategy, Bad Strategy*, and Frank Cespedes's *Aligning Strategy and Sales*. Each of them makes the case for a workable definition, proposing a slightly different angle. I'll go a step further than all of them by stripping things down to the essentials:

- Rumelt claims the kernel of a strategy contains three elements: a diagnosis, a guiding policy, and a coherent action. I find this definition too broad.

- Martin contends that strategy is a coordinated and integrated set of five choices: a winning aspiration, competitive parameters, competitive advantage, core capabilities, and management systems. I find this framework too elaborate for the purposes of selling.

- Cespedes believes that strategy boils down to objective, scope, and advantage. I like the simplicity of that definition, and I feel that we can streamline it even more.

Taking a seller's perspective, I believe you should be able to answer these two questions about your client: "Where do they compete?" and "How will they win?" If you can clearly define those two things, it's fair to say you understand their strategy. These questions embody a clear set of choices and trade-offs. Knowing where your client has chosen to compete requires you to understand which areas of the market they have deliberately excluded from consideration. Knowing how your client can win requires you to understand what distinguishes them from competitors. When you understand those elements, you can quickly figure out what matters to the business, and ideally how to demonstrate your value to a company buyer.

These two questions, while seemingly simple, are in fact very difficult for many businesses to answer. That is another reason why "strategic" conversations often fail to live up to their promise. Determining where to compete and how to win typically demands vigorous debate and careful deliberation. The easier and more common approach is simply to expand the scope of one's ambition in proportion to one's growing sense of what seems commercially possible. Strategists resist that temptation. They see clearly what they are giving up, and they accept the potential downside. They recognize what could be lost in choosing one path over another, but they embrace this choice because they believe that winning in the market requires an all-in focus. Compromise is seen as something that would undermine their competitive prospects.

As a seller, you should be attuned to your client's choices and trade-offs. You should be paying attention to the decision variables they are confronting. Even if the client is unclear on these choices, you should aspire to be. It may help to remind you what best-in-class strategic thinking looks like. Let's take a moment to review two of the most iconic examples from the modern business era, involving Steve Jobs and Jeff Bezos. Pay attention to the clarity of their decision-making process. Ask yourself what version of these discussions may have taken place in your client's conference room.

When Jobs returned to lead Apple in 1996, it was by no means obvious that he was destined to succeed. He had been abruptly ousted from the firm 11 years prior, on the heels of an unseemly power struggle. Since then, Apple leadership had overextended itself and the company was on the verge of bankruptcy, its stock sitting at less than a dollar per share. At the time, there were so many Apple product variations that consumers were getting confused. Sales had been declining for months.

Jobs's unusual strategic strength, according to biographer Walter Isaacson, was the ability to focus. "Deciding what not to do is as important as deciding what to do," Jobs is reported to have said. "That's true for companies, and it's true for products." His iconic turnaround moment was a boardroom session in 1997 with Apple's key technical leads, in which he reduced the complexity of their current product line to a simple matrix. Above two columns he wrote "Consumer" and "Pro." Beside the two intersecting rows, he wrote "Desktop" and "Portable." Apple's job, he said, was to make four great products—one for each quadrant. The audience was flabbergasted. Many of them were effectively being told that their babies were ugly. But that moment of truth was what started the company's fabled reversal of fortune.

Jobs had unambiguously addressed the first part of strategy (*Where do we compete?*) and he was just as clear on the second (*How do we win?*). The key to market dominance, he believed, was simplicity. This was more than a pragmatic calculation. It emerged from his own artistic disposition. Far from being just a canny marketing ploy, simplicity represented Jobs's philosophy on business and life:

> Why do we assume that simple is good? Because with physical products, we have to feel we can dominate them. As you bring order to complexity, you find a way to make the product defer to you. Simplicity isn't just a visual style. It's not just minimalism or the absence of clutter. It involves digging through the depth of the complexity. To

be truly simple, you have to go really deep. For example, to have no screws on something, you can end up having a product that is so convoluted and so complex. The better way is to go deeper with the simplicity, to understand everything about it and how it's manufactured. You have to deeply understand the essence of a product in order to be able to get rid of the parts that are not essential.

Jeff Bezos was also impressively clear about where to compete and how to win. But while Jobs leaned toward simplification, Bezos favored optimization. According to Brad Stone's excellent biography, *The Everything Store*, Bezos was fanatically methodical about everything. This becomes clear in reviewing the choices and trade-offs he made in deciding where Amazon should compete. His goal was always to create "The Everything Store," but his initial focus was on books. Of all the potential product categories, why were books the commercial beachhead for Amazon? What was the basis for taking such a highly specific first step? There were at least three reasons:

- *Substitutable Product:* Books are non-perishable commodities. A book in one store is practically identical to the same book carried in another. Buyers could plausibly be persuaded to purchase a book that interested them if a new entrant could materially reduce the retail price.

- *Dependable Supply:* There were two primary distributors of books in the US at that time, Ingram and Baker & Taylor, which accounted for the vast majority of distribution volume. A new retailer like Amazon wouldn't have to approach each of the thousands of book publishers individually. Bezos could depend on a simple and secure supply channel, allowing him to redefine the demand side of the book business.

- *Retail Opportunity:* At the time of Amazon's launch, there were more than 1.5 million English-language books in print, but even superstores couldn't stock more than 10 percent of those titles. As a digital platform, Amazon offered a way to eliminate most of the physical barriers to unlimited selection. In addition, Amazon could capture more value from millions of small-run books than from the few international bestsellers that were popular at any given time.[4]

That's how Bezos determined where to compete. Having carefully staked out a place in the market, he was equally intentional about how to win, specifying core competencies that would build and maintain a competitive advantage:

If you want to get to the truth about what makes us different, it's this: We are genuinely customer-centric, we are genuinely long-term oriented, and we genuinely like to invent. Most companies are not those things. They are focused on the competitor, rather than the customer. They want to work on things that will pay dividends in two or three years, and if they don't work in two or three years they will move on to something else. And they prefer to be close followers rather than inventors, because it's safer. So if you want to capture the truth about Amazon, that is why we are different. Very few companies have all of those three elements.[5]

Jobs and Bezos were especially thoughtful about where to compete and how to win as they built their respective behemoths. They were quintessential strategists. What can we learn from them as we think about selling to large companies? It comes back to what is most likely to get an executive buyer to see the value of what you bring to the table. The quickest way to prove value is through the lens of strategy. The human brain is associative, and if you can connect your agenda to what is familiar and top-of-mind for an executive, you stand a much better chance of getting their attention (*Does this matter?*). In addition, it will be much easier to get internal support for your initiative if it aligns with established priorities. Finally, understanding where your client competes and how they can win will immediately set you apart from other sellers. Thinking like a Strategist will help you detach from the emotive elements of the conversation, strengthening your credibility as a trusted advisor.

Building and sustaining a competitive advantage in the context of fast and fluid competition is a primary concern for your executive stakeholders. Sales professionals who seek to be taken seriously at the executive level must be capable of showing how their product or service supports a company's choices and trade-offs. For this reason, developing a Strategist mindset should be a professional development priority for those who seek to influence enterprise buyers. Our two key questions—"Where do they compete?" and "How will they win?"—take stock of the bigger picture and shrink it down to a manageable size. Such an approach might seem unattainable for many sales professionals, who often feel they don't have the time or ability to analyze an industry's structure in the way that Jobs and Bezos did. How does one tease out a client's strategy in an efficient and actionable way? The following chapters are designed to help. We'll explore three themes—target customer, value proposition, and priority metrics—to help us develop a bottom-up perspective on strategy. These alternative ways to think about your client's business will give you the means to demonstrate a Strategist mindset.

CHAPTER 2

Who Is Their Target Customer?

In answering the first of the two strategy questions—Where do they compete?—the easiest place to start is with the target customer. After all, the fundamental purpose of a business is, as management theorist Peter Drucker once said, to create a customer.[1] Your client's target customer is the keystone variable. It defines the competitive parameters of their business, and it has enormous influence on their allocation of company resources. Your most basic responsibility, then, is to figure out who buys from your customer and why.

I've always been impressed by the origin story of Airbnb and how it shows the importance of this point. In the beginning, Brian Chesky, Joe Gebbia, and Nathan Blecharczyk had only the faintest sense of what they were creating, based on positive but limited market feedback. True, they had been admitted to the prestigious Silicon Valley startup incubator, Y Combinator, on the strength of the founding team and their business plan. But, to borrow LinkedIn co-founder Reid Hoffman's famous analogy for entrepreneurship, they had jumped off a cliff and were building their airplane as they sped to the ground.

In a pivotal 2008 meeting with Y Combinator's founder, Paul Graham, the Airbnb founders shared the latest insights on their business. Apparently, there was burgeoning interest in the New York region, and particularly in the borough of Brooklyn. The founders were excitedly relaying this intelligence, but Graham looked perplexed. Eventually, he explained what wasn't sitting well with him. "Why," he asked, "are you guys talking to me in San Francisco if you've just declared that the center of gravity for your business is in New York? You need to get on the first plane and start talking to your customers over there. You need to find out what turned them into believers so that you can build on these insights."

They immediately did as he had suggested, conducting a series of face-to-face interviews with their early adopters on the East coast. These were deep and unconstrained discussions in which the founders looked at why the customers were drawn to the service and what would have made it a three-star, four-star, five-star … up to a ten-star experience. They made these customers feel special—hanging on their words and scrutinizing their photos—to come to a more nuanced understanding of what was working well, what was not, and where the opportunities for improvement stood out. They turned the weakness of a startup (lack of scale) into an enormous strength (customer intimacy). What they learned in those conversations proved instrumental to Airbnb's ultimate success.[2]

The principle for mature businesses is the same: Strategy is built around a clear understanding of the customer. Established businesses also need to know who buys from them and why. With this understanding they determine where to compete and how to win. It's important to note that for many large enterprises the customer is evolving, not just at the corporate level but for specific business units as well. For this reason, strategy is never fixed. It needs to adjust to market dynamics, which are perpetually in motion. To illustrate the importance of staying focused on the customer, consider the contrasting fortunes of Home Depot and McDonald's in the early 2000s.

McDonald's had enjoyed a 50-year growth record that was the envy of the retail sector, and a key factor had been their ability to stay dialed into the customer's perspective. Up until the early 2000s, in-store customers were not actually considered the *primary* customers for McDonald's. Multi-site real estate developers and franchise owners were. The company allocated significant resources to supporting the needs of these customers and sustained a growth trend over decades, with some 1,700 new McDonald's locations opening each year. By 2003, however, the tide had turned. In-store sales were declining, as people became less interested in the usual standardized fare. The decline in sales was sufficiently concerning that McDonald's brought in a new CEO, Jim Cantalupo, who immediately declared that "the new boss at McDonald's is the customer."[3] This prompted an immediate shift in corporate structure and resource allocation. McDonald's moved from a highly centralized model to one in which regional managers customized menus according to local tastes: green tea milkshakes in Japan and charcoal-grilled patties in Israel, for example. (I still recall the body-wide waves of bliss when I first devoured a McDonald's poutine at the end of a debauched evening in the Canadian province of Quebec.) The benefit of that shift was validated immediately and over the long term, with McDonald's being one of only two companies to register a stock price increase during the 2008–2009 financial crisis.

Home Depot responded very differently to the shifting sands across its customer base. Three years before Cantalupo took over at McDonald's, Home Depot recruited Bob Nardelli from GE as the new CEO. Home Depot seemed to be a wildly successful company, with a 20-year record of growth that had outpaced even Wal-Mart's, but there were financial and operational warning signs that needed to be quickly addressed. Nardelli's strategic choices were much less definitive than Cantalupo's. Nardelli acknowledged that the home improvement business was saturated, but he wasn't prepared to get out of it entirely. Instead, he kept one foot in their traditional customer base and simultaneously began catering to professional contractors, which he saw as a major growth opportunity. This decision also had a significant impact on resource allocation. Nardelli approved the layoff of thousands of customer service agents—the people who walk the floor in recognizable orange aprons—at 1,900 stores.

He took those savings and redirected them to an $8 billion acquisition spree, absorbing several wholesale housing supply companies. Revenues increased in the short term, but neither segment was served well, and customer satisfaction dropped more precipitously than for any other US retailer. Nardelli resigned after a six-year tenure.

The lessons above are not confined to business-to-consumer (B2C) businesses like McDonald's and Home Depot. B2B companies need to be just as responsive, and just as clear, in defining their primary customer. The evolution of LinkedIn is a good example. LinkedIn began as a platform solution, aspiring to be the world's largest social network for professionals, as well as a default search engine for people in a professional context. In the early years, it remained focused on those aspirations, steadily driving member growth and platform participation. The primary customer was the individual LinkedIn member, and the primary source of value was connecting members to economic opportunity through the power of network effects. Over time LinkedIn noticed there was an emerging customer: company recruiters. To capture this opportunity, LinkedIn created a new product (LinkedIn Recruiter) and built a B2B sales organization to pursue this market opportunity. Shortly thereafter it noted the emergence of another new customer: B2B sales professionals. This triggered the launch of a new product (LinkedIn Sales Navigator) and the creation of another field sales team. LinkedIn's evolution from a social network to a platform model that now operates in four distinct B2B verticals (recruiting, sales, marketing, and learning) shows how organic a company's strategy can be. But it also reinforces the importance of basing each strategic pivot on a clear understanding of the primary customer.

Let's go back to what these stories teach about strategy, and how they are relevant to the sales professional. Recall that strategy boils down to answering two questions: "Where do we compete?" and "How do we win?" Recall, as well, that you are much more likely to get the attention of executive buyers and influencers if you understand these two dimensions of their company. Knowing the target customer is the first and most important step in defining the competitive parameters of any business, because identifying a target customer requires choices and trade-offs. It forces you to sharpen your focus. It immediately provides clues as to what it will take for the business to win.

For all these reasons, you should prioritize the target customer in your initial research and discovery calls. Sales professionals who understand this dimension are best positioned to add value to a client's business. Sales professionals who lead with this mindset are more likely to be taken seriously at the executive level. But there are many aspects to a target customer's reality. It helps to have a framework to guide your questions and research. The next chapter goes a step further, giving you a more complete picture of the target customer's perspective so that you can think about where to align your product or service for maximum impact.

CHAPTER 3

How Does That Customer See the World?

Typically, sellers demonstrate empathy by showing they perceive and understand what the client is going through. That is unquestionably an important skill, and we'll return to it in Part III, but it's not part of a Strategist's toolkit for B2B selling. To be sure, empathy is important, but it's empathy for the *client's target customer* that matters most to the Strategist. The customer of your customer should be top of mind. If you can bring insight and practical guidance on how to win over that customer, you have earned a seat at the table for a genuinely strategic discussion. From the Strategist's point-of-view, empathy is about seeing the field through the target customer's eyes. It's about helping your client better serve that customer in a competitive context. Empathizing with the target customer is therefore one of the most effective ways to align your product or service with the client's strategic priorities.

How, then, do we empathize with the target customer? As in the previous chapter, I believe it's useful to look at the startup world as a source of principles that can be applied to the enterprise space. A founder who is looking to build a customer base from scratch must have a well-defined value proposition for the buyer. The do-or-die urgency of a startup company demands such clarity of focus. However, as we've seen with the examples from McDonald's, Home Depot, and LinkedIn, mature companies must also be refining their customer value proposition if they hope to stay relevant. If you have a systematic way to analyze your customer's value proposition, it gives you tremendous advantage in supporting them.

I believe Geoffrey Moore's *Crossing the Chasm* is the most practical reference here. Moore's book is predominantly for start-ups, but it contains important principles that apply to larger businesses as well. His overarching objective is to help founders navigate the "transition from an early market dominated by a few visionary customers to a mainstream market dominated by a large block of customers who are predominantly pragmatists in orientation." To that end, he lays out the key elements of success for any mainstream market, boiling these down to "a value proposition that can be predictably delivered to a targetable set of customers at a reasonable price."[1] It sounds elementary, but what exactly is a "value proposition"? As with the term "strategy," few people bother to investigate what these words really mean.

From a sales perspective, there are good reasons to have a detailed grasp of the concept. Understanding your client's value proposition is the most rigorous way to delineate where they compete and how they can win. Moore proposes a simple, two-sentence formula for building out any customer value proposition. It goes like this:

> For [target customers] … who are dissatisfied with [the current market alternative] our product is a [product category] … that provides [compelling reason to buy]. Unlike [the product alternative], we have assembled [key whole product features for your specific application]. [2]

Imagine how credible you would be if you could articulate these elements on behalf of your customer. It would prove that you had taken the time to properly understand their business. It would give them confidence that you've put their priorities above your own. For your most important clients especially, I believe it is well worth the investment of time to familiarize yourself with their value proposition. The exercise will significantly improve your ability to bring an objective mindset to the conversation. Here's how I've re-engineered the six components of Moore's two sentence formula, making them practical parts of a seller's diagnosis:

1. *Problem:* What problem does your client solve?

2. *Customer:* Who is your client's primary buyer?

3. *Positioning:* How will that buyer frame your client's product or service?

4. *Alternatives:* To what other product/service will the target buyer compare your client's offering?

5. *Differentiation:* What are your client's competitive advantages/disadvantages?

6. *Integrations:* What are indirect benefits for the target buyer of using your client's product/service?

Given all the pressures of the job, sellers are understandably tempted to gloss over such details. In forecast and coaching discussions, it's common for them to reach for shorthand characterizations of what their clients do: "They're a SaaS company"; "They're an industrial manufacturer"; "They do commercial lending." But the most successful salespeople are those who legitimately help the client solve a problem. To be capable of that, you need a framework for breaking down the client's business and identifying their most salient challenges in the market. The customer value proposition provides a construct for thinking about how to strengthen their competitive position. It helps to maintain your objectivity in evaluating how to support them.

Let's make this as practical as possible. Let's assume that you're a B2B sales professional and your software records video and phone conversations between salespeople and their customers. It's a "conversational intelligence solution" to support coaching and mentoring across the sales organization. Let's further assume that you're selling to a cybersecurity firm and that you're developing your perspective on how to help them. We'll use the customer value proposition framework to analyze the client's business, and then we'll consider how this exercise might inform your approach to discovery calls.

Our hypothetical cybersecurity firm—Darius, Musashi, & Zulu, or DMZ—sells to business buyers, everything from small to large companies. Broadly speaking, they divide their business into products and services. Products are hardware and software components of a company's security infrastructure, such as wireless networking or web filtering. Services can be anything from subscription-based threat detection to technical support to IT consultation to training. Let's now work through the six components of the customer value proposition so we can prepare a sales thesis.

1. PROBLEM: What problem does your client solve?

I cannot overstate the importance of knowing the underlying business problem and what's unique about the way your client solves it. For any business, nothing is more fundamental than the problem they have identified, and how they are uniquely positioned to address it. I find that asking them directly—literally, "What problem do you solve?"—creates an immediate connection with someone on the client side. It draws attention to their core reason for being, reinforcing a sense of collective purpose. In this case the problem is straightforward and compelling: Modern businesses are highly vulnerable to cybercriminal activities, such as hacking, data theft, and industrial espionage. DMZ is confronting what looks like an urgent necessity for many companies today.

2. CUSTOMER: Who is your client's primary buyer?

As you research DMZ, you are initially confused about who the target customer is. You learn that, historically, most of DMZ's sales have been through managed security system providers (MSSPs). In other words, they have traditionally sold to channel partners, who in turn have sold to end-users. However, as you continue to read the DMZ annual report, you note that this reliance on indirect selling is now perceived as a business risk. DMZ leadership believes that growth, particularly within the enterprise space, will require brand- and relationship-building with end-users. Based on this information, you conclude that their target customer has evolved to become the Chief Information Security Officer (CISO) of these end-users. The CISO appears to be the critical decision-maker for unlocking DMZ's growth potential—especially in the enterprise space. Therefore, you resolve to understand how the CISO is likely to view market alternatives so that you can help DMZ position itself most advantageously.

3. POSITIONING: How will that buyer frame your client's product or service?

Moore claims that "positioning is the single largest influence on the buying decision. It serves as a kind of buyers' shorthand, shaping not only their final choice but even the way they evaluate alternatives leading up to that choice."[3] It is critical, then, to understand how your customer frames their product or service. You want to ensure you're not inadvertently diminishing their value proposition. I remember getting my hand slapped by a client once because I referred to their product as a "tool." The client sternly reminded me that they were selling a "platform," not a "tool." He explained that "tool" suggested a narrow instrumental purpose, while "platform" conveyed the idea of an ecosystem whose value is proportional to the degree of user engagement. DMZ's positioning seems clear enough: They offer complete cyber protection of a company's digital attack surface.

4. ALTERNATIVES: To what other product/service will the target buyer compare your client's offering?

As you continue to investigate this industry, you start to see just how overwhelmed the CISO must be. Cybersecurity has become a mission-critical concern for many businesses, and CISOs are experiencing a deluge of overtures from new and established firms. The CISO is likely going to divide the current alternatives into three camps: (1) large incumbent IT and networking providers that augment existing contracts with a wide range of cybersecurity options; (2) cybersecurity firms with a full spectrum of products and services; and (3) specialized vendors that focus on specific areas of the attack surface, such as data protection, identity management, or Internet of Things (IoT). DMZ appears to fall into the second category.

5. DIFFERENTIATION: What are your client's competitive advantages/disadvantages?

This point requires a call-back to the target customer's options defined in the previous point (To what other product/service will the target buyer compare your client's offering?). What does DMZ do better than the current market alternatives? Based on further reading of the "competition" section of DMZ's annual report, as well as other online research, you start to piece together what matters to the CISO:

- *Reliability:* Performance must be practically error-free, given the cost of failure.

- *Interoperability:* Solutions must be compatible with the existing IT infrastructure.

- *Adaptability:* Vendors need to stay ahead of the rapid evolution in cyber threats.

- *Compliance:* Vendors must meet the rigorous demands of highly regulated industries.

- *Cost:* Vendors must minimize the total cost of ownership.

Your research and initial calls with DMZ employees indicate that they compare favorably against the competition in the areas of Reliability, Adaptability, Compliance, and Cost. Interoperability is a potential weakness, however, because they are up against massive incumbents in IT and networking, whose product range far exceeds that of DMZ. These competitors also have much bigger marketing budgets and brand recognition. You start to think about how DMZ can maximize its strengths in such a competitive context.

6. INTEGRATIONS: What are indirect benefits of using your client's product/service?

There could be a range of indirect benefits to DMZ customers. Given the extent of DMZ services, you suspect that they could streamline customer spend by consolidating previously disparate IT projects. You also suspect there could be indirect operational benefits because, by minimizing disruption, DMZ might enhance productivity in the client's core operations. This part of the value proposition requires you to explore areas in which your client's solution creates synergies with the surrounding processes and technologies.

Now that you've come to a better understanding of DMZ's business, you need to think about how to frame the potential value of your product—which, as a reminder, is a software solution that records video and phone conversations between salespeople and their clients. Your target customer at DMZ is their VP of Sales because she has the greatest stake in your solution. Let's do a quick A/B comparison to illustrate the difference between a talk track grounded in the above strategic analysis versus a more conventional approach. For the conventional approach, some of your key messages might be as follows:

> Our technology gathers conversational intelligence from thousands of interactions between your customers and DMZ sellers each day. You can use this intelligence to

improve your coaching, sharpen your revenue forecasts, and detect shifts in the competitive landscape. Our technology easily integrates with your video and teleconferencing platforms, and numerous third-party reviews confirm that we meet global privacy and security standards. Some of the world's most recognizable companies are using our solution, and we continue to receive glowing reviews from them. Our growth rate illustrates just how quickly our solution is catching on in the sales industry. We believe we can rapidly advance DMZ's strategic agenda.

What makes this approach "conventional" is that it is squarely rooted in your product's features and benefits, with DMZ's strategy included only as an afterthought. These are enticing features and benefits, to be sure, but they lose much of their potential impact by skipping over the client's strategy. Let's now consider how a strategic pitch might be designed instead:

We understand that DMZ is competing in a hotly contested space. We also understand that you are up against well-established IT and network providers with greater brand recognition and larger marketing budgets. As you shift your focus from indirect sellers to end-users in the enterprise segment, we suspect there will be new challenges for the sales team. Capturing and sustaining the attention of CISOs is extremely hard, especially for salespeople who traditionally weren't expected to do so. And yet your growth will depend on better engagement with these buyers, since they are the primary stakeholders for cybersecurity solutions in the enterprise segment.

We think we can help you adapt to this new reality. With greater visibility into thousands of daily sales calls, our conversational intelligence solution will quickly identify what the top performers are doing, so that you can scale these practices across the team. We will also uncover new themes that emerge in client discussions, so that you and the leadership team can pre-empt them. In short, we can accelerate the development of your sales talent and help you anticipate new challenges and opportunities in your target market. That's why we believe we can rapidly advance DMZ's strategic agenda.

Did you feel the greater persuasion in the second approach? It's not as though the first approach was useless. The features and benefits of this hypothetical solution speak for themselves. They are inherently attractive, and you can probably imagine a context in which a mid-level manager, particularly someone from IT, might be tempted to respond to a salesperson's outreach. But the second approach is on another level. It shows deep empathy for the business. It covers themes that are more likely to be familiar to an executive decision-maker. It speaks to what matters to DMZ's new target buyer.

This is what I mean by adopting the mindset of a Strategist. When you adopt that mindset, you visualize your audience very differently. You think of yourself as someone who belongs at the table where strategic decisions are made. You no longer diminish yourself by assuming that such decisions are above your head or pay grade. To achieve this elevated view, you simply need to prioritize the end customer's perspective. The customer value proposition framework supports this discipline in a structured and systematic way. It's a deeply empathetic approach to sales, but the empathy is grounded in a focus on external dynamics that impact the client's target buyer. Taking this approach improves your credibility as a trusted advisor because it helps you depersonalize the interaction. You and your client can assess the variables that are objectively important to their business. Most sellers will not do this. It will seem absurdly demanding. But those who embrace a Strategist mindset will always stand out from the crowd. You need to decide which game you want to play.

CHAPTER 4

How Do They Measure Success?

I remember a challenging sale with an established telecom client. The firm was operating in a mature industry with very few competitors. Even if it exceeded annual projections, the company growth rate was still in the low single digits. Our sales team had been trying for years to get on the calendar of the executive team. We had been repeatedly rebuffed and diverted to the middle management level. Achieving strategic alignment as we've discussed in the previous chapters was proving to be exceptionally difficult. There was no charismatic leader who had announced a bold, market-making initiative. There were only the smallest cracks of daylight between this company's value proposition and that of its few competitors. We felt stuck.

The situation finally shifted when we started to learn how the executive leadership team was measuring success. They viewed the business as a kind of engineering puzzle, and they were preoccupied with tracking internal processes front to back, putting singular emphasis on a few metrics that had a disproportionate impact on their bottom line. You could say they were productivity hawks. We looked at how these senior leaders were measuring the sales process, and we learned they had calculated a 50 percent win-rate for proposals—in other words, about half their proposals created revenue for the business because of the small number of competitors in the market. This immediately focused our sales efforts. It became clear that we could significantly boost the client's sales performance if we improved the team's efficiency and effectiveness prior to the proposal stage. In theory, a 20 percent increase in proposal volume could yield a 10 percent increase in company revenue.

Our team met with our primary sponsors in middle management, and we all rolled up our sleeves to agree on the key activities that would impact proposal volume. We discussed several possibilities but ultimately focused only on those that we could measurably impact. This gave us a fact base to establish the current baseline and set performance targets for our team. Collaborating with our client counterparts, we put together a proposal to improve the client's prospecting and qualification processes. That was the point at which we were finally successful in getting the executive leadership team's attention.

Here, again, was an instance of approaching the client with a different mindset. Up until this point in the relationship we had been put in a box. We had occupied the dismissible cat-egory of "vendor," failing to distinguish ourselves from the many other technology solution providers. But we refused to accept this label, and we started to act like a partner. We assumed we had a stake in their business, and that we were committed to their success as much as our own. However, we needed a hook. In the absence of a dominant internal narrative around which we could rally, we had to look at the nuts and bolts of their business. As with the customer value proposition, we had to take a bottom-up approach. In this case, we had to figure out what was getting the most oper-ational attention.

Internal metrics can be another effective route for the Strategist because they implicitly convey where the client plays and how they expect to win. Key metrics are import-ant to mature industries in which competitors tend to advance in inches rather than yards. They are also vital to young companies building a new culture and perhaps even a new market. (Think of the early years of Amazon, during which inventory turnovers, customer returns, and purchases per visit were carefully tracked while operating profit was largely ignored.) Hard choices and trade-offs are captured in the few critical metrics that are called out among the many trivial ones. Strategists make it a priority to seek out such metrics and to use them to inform their sales effort.

The obvious question is: Which metrics deserve your attention? A good way to think about this is through the lens of a concept called "objectives and key results" (OKRs). It was first described in a book called *Measure What Matters* by John Doerr, a long-time advisor to Google and many of the biggest names in Silicon Valley. OKRs are inspired by the "Big Rocks Theory," first popularized in *The 7 Habits of Highly Effective People* by Stephen Covey. Imagine you have some rocks, some pebbles, and some sand, and you've been asked to fit them all into a wide-mouthed jar. If you first add the sand, then the pebbles, and finally the big rocks, you'll find that the rocks don't fit. But if you start with the big rocks, then add the pebbles, the sand fills the remaining gaps in the jar. It's a powerful metaphor that underlines the importance of doing the most important things first.

An OKR analysis can be an efficient way to identify a senior leader's key concern (*Does this matter?*). OKRs are strategic in that they require hard choices. They eliminate confusion and provide collective focus on what's needed to win. They function as a team compass and baseline for ongoing performance assessment. Objectives are the big rocks representing the overarching goals of the business you are working with. These are the "what." Key results are the pebbles and sand. They are measurable outcomes that bring the client closer to their overarching goal. These are the "how." Applying the OKR filter to your customer's business, you should set out to find the dominant objective and a few associated key results.

This was the approach we took with our telecom client. Bear in mind that the concept of OKRs was foreign to them. It wasn't part of their company vocabulary. Nonetheless, OKRs were the basis of our first-principles approach, helping us identify the business opportunity. We asked about the metrics they were tracking. We asked how these were related to metrics that mattered most to management.

OKR logic guided our exploratory discussion, and we charted out the primary drivers of their proposal process in a visual way. We also identified the current baseline measures against each of the key results, so that our team could set quantifiable improvement targets against them. See Figure 4.1 for a simplified version of our assessment:

Figure 4.1

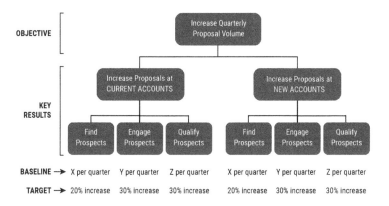

The overarching objective was to increase proposal volume. The key results were measurable prospecting outcomes that contributed to this goal. Our simple framework was the basis of a pilot initiative and future business case. More importantly, it was the primary mechanism for getting executive decision-makers to pay attention. We had finally proved that we understood what mattered to them, and soon we had a story about what we believed could be improved.

OKRs were the tip of the spear, so to speak. They allowed us to pierce the armor protecting the senior team. More importantly, though, they set us up for deeper collaboration with the client. We became a valuable partner in executive discussions because we had linked our solution to their business strategy. We now had a role in supporting their OKR agendas. Suddenly, the client was interested in what we had learned from our discovery conversations with field management and frontline users. By speaking their language, we had earned their trust. That was sufficient to transform our outsider status into a source of strength. They wanted to know what we had learned in our research, and they were open to our findings and recommendations because we had now achieved credible detachment.

In fact, much of our value to the client was rooted in our unique perspective as sellers. This is worth expanding upon because it gets to the heart of how salespeople can often add value. In most businesses there is some type of communication breakdown from the executive level to the field ranks. Few executive leaders are truly confident in their understanding of what's happening several layers below them. Many have an unspoken fear of being perceived as out-of-touch. This feature of executive psychology is what salespeople are singularly capable of addressing. The seller as Strategist plays the role of a go-between, bridging the divide between silos and hierarchical rungs. As businesses become more complex, salespeople become more valuable as a sensing mechanism. If properly positioned, their discovery findings can be a source of business insight. Armed with such insights, the seller can facilitate collaboration within the client organization, helping people and divisions talk to each other more effectively.

OKRs are a powerful construct to enable such collaboration. That's because OKRs are not meant to be islands.

They are designed to tie to other areas of the company, and the Strategist can raise the profile of a sales initiative by revealing such interdependencies. In the case of our telecom client, we focused on prospecting measures to increase the number of potential buyers for the sales team. That got the attention of marketing colleagues in the client's organization because these colleagues were looking to drive customer interest through virtual seminars and events. Suddenly they wanted to learn more about our solution, and they asked to be included in the pilot initiative. When it ultimately came time to present our business case to the executive team, we had a more diversified group of advocates supporting us. OKR discussions were the forcing function that helped to create this broader coalition.

As business continues to evolve from being largely top-down to increasingly network-based, sellers should be more conscious of their boundary-crossing role. They should also note the potential of OKR discussions to support the negotiation of these company boundaries. Good ideas are no longer confined to the top of the hierarchy, and often the most powerful and motivating OKRs emerge from front-line contributions. Indeed, within the modern knowledge economy, innovation is more distributed than centralized. The power and potential of salespeople is that they can see organizational gaps and interconnections, often more easily than employees can. OKR validation can support such discoveries. They can uncover fresh stakeholders and perspectives across the business, creating new paths to value.

As with the customer value proposition, OKRs provide a set of conversational guardrails to support your discovery.

They also create the opportunity to build trust through objectivity. As we've seen, not all businesses are explicitly committed to OKRs, but all businesses lend themselves to an OKR analysis. That is why Doerr provides such a wide range of examples in *Measure What Matters*, from Bono to Bill Gates. The OKR frame is powerful in its simplicity, forcing you to narrow a range of potential priorities down to the essential few. Such a discipline has two benefits for you as the seller. First, it forces you to focus on what is most likely to get an executive's attention. Second, it establishes quantifiable evaluation criteria, shortening the distance to your plausible objectivity as a seller.

Let's take stock of where we are on our learning path. Becoming a Strategist requires a mindset shift. Sellers who make this shift start to see themselves and their relationship to the client in a fundamentally different way. Essentially, Strategists attempt to fortify the client's competitive advantage. They use simple frameworks to reduce the client's operational complexity into manageable elements. Strategists assume they belong in executive conversations, but they also know they must prove they've earned this right. They're acutely aware that executives have many more reasons to ignore salespeople than to pay attention to them, so they relentlessly seek out the things that matter. They establish who the target customer is. They stand in the shoes of that customer to understand how they would evaluate the client's product or service. They uncover the client's overarching OKRs. Like an investigative journalist, they seek out truths that are hidden and obscured in organizational silos.

The frameworks and approaches we've covered are the tools and skills that support this mindset shift. They are the practical and tactical means of acting out a more elevated version of what it means to sell. To transcend the limits of mere likeability or mutuality, you must be able to detach and see the field. That means becoming an engaged student of your client's business, so you can challenge, educate, and ideally collaborate with the customer. That is what Strategists set out to do, and it's what these frameworks should allow. They're intended to help organize your analysis, support a stronger working relationship, and ultimately drive action. They are the rudiments of strategy for those who influence corporate buyers.

It may now help you to see how these principles play out in an actual sale. To bring them to life, let me share the story of how a top-performing sales professional learned to become a Strategist.

CHAPTER 5

The Strategist in Action

Emily had just started as a senior salesperson with a company that sold an innovative B2B software solution to simplify content storage, search, and retrieval. On Day 1 she pledged to approach her sales process very differently. She was tired of simply working through a list of to-dos. She was fed up with not having carved out "thinking time" to develop a richer understanding of the client's operating environment. This time she wouldn't compromise. From the start of her tenure, she was determined to sell differently in her new role.

Emily felt especially sure that this was the right approach when she learned which clients were in her territory. They were some of the largest, most recognized companies in the world. If she had any hope of working with them effectively, she needed to be extremely thoughtful and strategic in how she engaged with senior stakeholders.

The first thing Emily did was immerse herself in the investor relations section of the website for one of her most important clients, a global tech firm that sells hardware, software, and consulting services. The investor relations page was surprisingly easy to navigate. Many of the documents were clearly intended for the common shareholder, not for quant jocks intent on performing a spreadsheet analysis.

One of the first things Emily noticed was the transcript from a call in which her client's senior executive team fielded questions from industry analysts. At a certain point in the transcript, one of the analysts asked something along the lines of "Why do clients buy from you?" A member of the C-suite was the first to weigh in, and he gave three reasons. He said customers buy from them because they are innovative, because of their commitment to trust and safety, and because they offer a global team of trusted advisors.

The third point seemed like an important insight. Thinking about the basics of strategy, Emily didn't yet have a clear sense of who the target customer was for such a sprawling and complex global firm. However, based on what she had just heard, she felt she understood what the client's leadership team considered to be their competitive advantage. Moreover, she now had a testable claim that she could validate by speaking to people on the front lines.

So that's what Emily set out to do. She wanted to establish whether the client's consulting team believed they had what they needed to establish themselves as "trusted advisors." It occurred to her that consulting revenue had to be dependent on proposal efficiency, as well as execution quality and speed. She asked herself how content management might be relevant to these capabilities. She hypothesized that quick and customized content delivery would probably be important to winning new business and maximizing the value of global knowledge assets in live engagements. She wanted to hear directly from the consulting teams whether this was a reasonable supposition. If it turned out to be the case, she also wanted to know whether they felt there were any shortcomings in the current content management system. Validating these hypotheses would be critical to determining whether she had something valuable to offer.

So Emily made contact with company consultants at the individual contributor and manager level. She confirmed her hypothesis that effective content management was a key capability that supported business development and value delivery. She also heard from many teams that knowledge assets were poorly organized and difficult to access when they were needed most. She soon learned there was a "last mile" problem. The company was like a Michelin-starred restaurant with master chefs and high-quality ingredients, but with no coordinated approach for food preparation, and no real feedback apart from tips on the check. She could see that the status quo was preventing members of the consulting team from being trusted advisors. Knowledge within the firm had become too tribal. This was the core insight that laid the foundations for a strategic sale.

Emily began to assemble the different pieces of her pitch. She had evidence from the client's investor relations materials that there was a clear go-to-market strategy. But her detective work had uncovered a gap between those public pronouncements and the reality on the ground. If she was going to call out this gap, the supporting materials had to be rigorous and unassailable.

She started with verbatim testimonials that came from the various teams she had spoken to. Next, she returned to publicly available documents, exploring additional analyst materials on the client's performance. She homed in on commentary related to the consulting business, noticing that many analysts were giving the client high marks for its technology, but questioning their performance in consulting services. Wall Street had observed that consulting sales were anemic in comparison to the technology business. Emily dug a little further and came across a third-party report that noted the disconnect between the company's avowed strategy and its internal capability.

She even searched for YouTube and podcast episodes that featured members of the executive team. These media appearances gave her a better feel for their personalities, and the more in-depth nature of these resources revealed nuances in their perspective on market challenges, supplementing what she had learned from more traditional research materials.

Emily now had the elements of a storyline to show that there was a strategic problem clearly in need of attention. She had anecdotal evidence from the field, as well as industry analysis to support those claims. She put together a deck that organized this information into simple plot points:

- You have indicated that your market performance depends on three core competencies.

- We evaluated the third competency—being trusted advisors—by speaking directly with your consulting teams.

- They identified several factors that undermine their ability to be trusted advisors.

- Ineffective and inefficient knowledge management emerged as a central theme.

- We have studied this problem with other large advisory firms and have a market-leading solution to address it.

These were the bare bones of her pitch, supplemented with quotes from the field and selected insights from industry reports. Emily sent the pitch to several leaders in the organization, and she quickly got a response from an executive in the marketing organization. The pitch tied in nicely with this person's own concerns that much of the best content from the marketing team hadn't been effectively distributed via the consulting teams. He felt this was preventing them from communicating the true value of the organization to the customer.

This connection got the ball rolling. Emily's storyline was solid, and it gave this marketing leader a legitimate strategic framework to become her ally. The executive was happy to shore up Emily's case, and to introduce her to a variety of other stakeholders so that they could build broader consensus in support of a buying decision. The executive knew that many advocates would be required to raise the profile of this initiative. The strength of Emily's core insight, together with the power of her storyline, gave him the comfort to grant Emily a "license to hunt" internally. He encouraged her to use his name as a reference in further outreach and education. This was a critical element that expedited the propagation of her key messages.

The road to a closed sale was long and winding, but eventually Emily and the client got there. Within Emily's firm, this was one of the largest sales in their history. It was a Roger Banister[1] moment that set a new benchmark for an enterprise deal. For Emily, one of the most satisfying elements was that it validated her instincts on how to sell properly. She had put in the time and unearthed a nugget of insight that guided all her subsequent efforts. It was validation of the strategic thinking she felt was vital to becoming a more trusted advisor to her clients.

Emily looks back on this sale as a threshold-crossing experience in her evolution as a sales professional. In the years leading up to it, she had exclusively relied on empathy, charm, and win-win visioning with her customers. This approach had been generally successful, but it achieved no more than incremental growth with her accounts. She once cited "busyness" as the key constraint, but the truth was that she was intimidated by the thought of engaging executives. She wasn't confident she could credibly engage them. This sale helped to demystify the executive ranks for her. She realized that executives speak to investors in the kind of simple language one uses to describe the Internet to a grandparent. She also saw that strategic insights are the prime mover for any transformational initiative. Her learnings from this experience have fundamentally reshaped her mindset, making her much more self-assured as a sales professional. She illustrates what it means to become a Strategist.

TAKEAWAYS FOR THE STRATEGIST

The Strategist mindset prioritizes factors that strengthen the client's competitive positioning. Here are the key points.

Client's Overall Strategy

- Where do they compete?
  - ➤ How are they defining their competitive space?
  - ➤ What is explicitly in and out of scope for this business?
- How will they win?
  - ➤ What are their relative strengths?
  - ➤ How can you and your company reinforce those strengths?

Client's Target Customer

- Who is the client's primary buyer?
- How and why has their primary buyer changed, if at all?

Client's Value Proposition

1. *Problem:* What problem does your client solve?
2. *Customer:* Who is your client's primary buyer?

3. *Positioning:* How will that buyer frame your client's product or service?
4. *Alternatives:* To what other product/service will the target buyer compare your client's offering?
5. *Differentiation:* What are your client's competitive advantages/disadvantages?
6. *Integrations:* What are indirect benefits of using your client's product/service?

Their Objectives and Key Results

- What are the most important objectives for the area of the client's business that you're working with?
- What are the key results (not just activities) that will advance those objectives?

Your Sales Thesis

- Where are the gaps between your client's strategic priorities—stated or implied—and their current capabilities?
- How could your product or service help to close these gaps?

PART II: BECOMING A CHANGE AGENT

*"Taking a new step, uttering a new word,
is what people fear most."*

—FYODOR DOSTOEVSKY

CHAPTER 6

Where Is the Energy?
How Can You Feed It?

I confess I had an especially pitiful addiction to the Netflix series *Breaking Bad*. Initially sensing the degree of my susceptibility to its diabolical charms, I put off watching the show until many years after the five seasons had been released. Finally, in a moment of weakness, I yielded to temptation, thinking I would "just sample a single episode." Eight hours later, at 4:00 a.m., I sat mouth agape in front of the TV, cursing my lack of willpower. The vicious cycle repeated each night for another two or three weeks until, bleary-eyed and begrudgingly, I completed the series.

But there were nuggets of wisdom I gleaned from this otherwise squandered time. (It's possible to rationalize anything, isn't it?) As we reflect on the nature of change, I can't help but recall the opening scene of *Breaking Bad*. Walter

White is addressing a class of openly disinterested high school students. Seeking a creative way to engage them, he opines that "Chemistry is the study of ... well, technically it's the study of matter. But I prefer to see it as the study of change." He becomes increasingly animated after lighting a Bunsen burner and spraying different substances into the flame to create a variety of visual effects, illustrating how elements combine and change into compounds. He then pauses to reflect on the broader meaning, saying: "That's all part of life, right? It's the constant. It's the cycle. It's solution and dissolution, just over and over again. It is growth, then decay, then transformation. It is fascinating, really."[1]

Yes, it is fascinating. Wharton Professor Jonah Berger—a world-renowned expert on how products, ideas, and behaviors catch on—would agree. In his book *The Catalyst: How to Change Anyone's Mind*, he makes the point that changing humans is more like chemistry than physics. In physics, you overcome resistance by applying more force.[2] If an object is too heavy, for example, you simply push harder. But that isn't how it works with human beings. People are not chairs to be shoved aside and rearranged on a whim. They change through a process reminiscent of "catalysis" in chemistry—adding a small amount of a certain substance can dramatically alter the rate at which chemical compounds undergo the process of transformation. Walter White was absolutely correct.

Becoming a change agent therefore starts with recognizing that one can't force change. Rather, one must seek to remove barriers, allowing change to happen. Change agents look at a client organization and ask two key questions:

Where is the energy for change coming from? and *How can I feed that energy?* An ability to feed and direct energy requires a clear understanding of the resistance you are up against. So, let's look at one of the most formidable barriers to change for the sales professional.

Appreciating this barrier requires an exercise in deep empathy. I first undertook such an exercise as part of an online course called the altMBA, created by entrepreneur, author, speaker, and famed marketing guru Seth Godin. One of the assignments was to perform a deep-dive on the customer's point of view when it came to their resistance to buying our product or service. The point was not to prepare ourselves for a range of possible objections so that we could eventually respond to them with stronger counterclaims. Rather, we were asked to fully embrace the needs and priorities of the client, to imagine that their resistance was not only reasonable but *heroic*. We were being called upon to participate in the customer's emotional reality, to see the pictures in their head, and to fully embrace their side in opposing our own interests. It's not an easy thing to do.

I pretended I was a "typical" tech salesperson, convinced of my product or service's "transformational" potential. Then I wrote a hypothetical rejection email from a sales prospect, doing my best to accentuate their virtue and imagine my potential blind spots:

> Hi Doug,
>
> Thank you for the video call the other day in which you introduced the team and shared your perspective. With all due respect, I'd like to suggest we go our separate ways at this point. Here's why:

First, we prefer to limit the changes we're imposing on our team. Our company now has several large-scale initiatives underway across the business. People are overwhelmed. Our job as a management team is to protect them from unnecessary increases in their workload. In fact, it's one of my primary responsibilities as a leader to limit distractions and ensure people can perform their best on mission-critical priorities. We don't have the luxury of a double-digital growth rate like yours. This is not the tech industry, and we need to fight for every additional percentage point of growth we can achieve. It really isn't a good time to be launching yet another "transformation" initiative. We must first deliver on our commitments to the executive team.

I should also mention the headspace of the people for whom you've proposed this initiative. Many of them are not millennials. It's not as if they can't wait to try out new technologies. These are people who value their autonomy and have refined processes that have proven to be successful. They don't take kindly to our unilaterally announcing new and allegedly better ways of doing their job. These folks are practical people who have figured out what works for them. There is almost no chance they will be receptive to yet another "disruptive technology" we introduce if they haven't asked for it. It would almost certainly be a waste of their time and the company's money.

I also have to say it's a little rich of you to talk about our need for change. If we were to buy your product, it would pose almost no risk to you. The sale would be only revenue upside from your perspective. We, on the other hand, would take full responsibility from the moment we signed the contract. We would have to carefully monitor the team. We would have to drive behavior change. We would have to measure and manage hundreds of people to ensure we made this a worthwhile investment. And we would have to do all these things on top of other high-priority programs that I already mentioned are in full flight. Yes, I recognize you have a support team, but we both know how this works. You are incentivized to maximize your revenue for the rest of the quarter or fiscal year. It's in your interest to de-prioritize this relationship once the contract ink is dry. We would be in a very different situation.

Finally, please consider this: It's nice that you've brought such youthful enthusiasm to our interactions. But we're going through some tough times at the moment. Frankly, your bright and smiling faces felt a little fake to us. It must be nice to have deep pockets and prestigious investors backing you, just in case your company needs a lifeline. We are not in such a position. Things are very serious right now. A cheerleading spirit might be part of the air you breathe, but for some of us on the call it was a little suffocating.

Anyway, I appreciated the time and effort you put into preparing for the meeting, which is why I'm returning the favor with such candid feedback. I know that honesty can sometimes be a bitter pill to swallow, but I firmly believe it helps all of us improve.

Best regards,

[Customer Hero]

To be quite clear, that was not an actual customer email. But I found it was a fascinating exercise to go through, because it forced me to visualize the full extent of a client's noble misgivings. I walked away with a much better sense of what makes up the primary psychological barrier for B2B sales professionals. I believe there are two sides to this barrier.

First, on the client's side, there is something that the behavioral economics community calls "present bias," or the tendency to overweight the present and to discount the future. Humans have a natural aversion to immediate costs and a natural blindness to longer-term effects. The prototypical illustration of this phenomenon comes from Homer Simpson, whose wife, Marge, once advised him that "someday these kids will be out of the house, and you'll regret not spending more time with them." Homer waves off her warning by saying, "That's a problem for future Homer. And *man*, I don't envy that guy!" He then pours vodka into a mayonnaise jar, shakes it vigorously, and downs the mix in one gulp before collapsing on the floor.[3] The client's default is to oppose anything that involves short-term pain, even in light of future benefits, because prospective gains are discounted while current costs loom large.

Second, on the side of the sales professional, there's a predictable way we often distort the client's motivation for resistance. This falls into the category of what psychologists call a "fundamental attribution error," or the human tendency to assign blame or credit to people for actions that are better explained by circumstances. We're often tempted to villainize those who oppose our agenda, speculating that they are too old-fashioned, too mean-spirited, or too simple-minded to see the truth as we see it. The reality, however, is that accepting the need for change is first and foremost a situation problem, not a people problem. It's crucial to understand the surrounding variables that shape a client's response.

As with the preceding discussion about strategy, this section is grounded in the importance of mindset. Your mindset profoundly shapes your behavior and performance. The same is true with your clients, which is why, through-out *The Sales MBA*, we always begin with an assessment of the client's mental frame. When we discussed strategy, we began by grounding ourselves in two critical features of an executive buyer's psychology: *Does this matter?* and *How is it going?* We looked at principles and approaches to address this frame of mind. When it comes to driving organiza-tional change, "present bias" is the equivalent starting point for your client. It is the baseline psychological reality you need to confront.

Beyond an accurate assessment of the customer, we need to elevate our own self-regard. This is why I began this sec-tion with a chemistry analogy. The central theme of this analogy is that Change Agents let change happen, rather than force it through, by eliminating barriers and allowing "catalysis" to run its course. Becoming a Change Agent requires us to see the invisible elements at play, and to understand what has shaped our client's resistance, often for perfectly understandable reasons. Change Agents learn how to minimize institutional drag. They see how to "sell past the sale" so that the future appears less risky and onerous to the buyer. It helps to have a framework for managing the organizational variables that matter most, and that's what we'll focus on over the coming chapters.

CHAPTER 7

Why Do We Change?

As one might expect, the literature on how to drive organizational change is vast and varied. I believe two books stand out as the most helpful. The first is *Switch* by Chip and Dan Heath. The second, which clearly inspired the first, is *Influencer: The New Science of Leading Change* by Joseph Grenny, Kerry Patterson, and others. I'll summarize the conceptual foundations of these books, then move to practical applications in the following chapters.

As we've discussed, catalysis in chemistry involves introducing small amounts of a certain substance to accelerate the process of transformation. Extensive studies on organizational change suggest three "chemical elements" propel such transformation: personal interests, social influences, and structural surroundings. A visual way to understand these elements is by way of a beautiful metaphor that I first encountered in Jonathan Haidt's book *The Happiness Hypothesis*.

Haidt argues that human behavior can best be understood through the image of a rider, an elephant, and a path. The rider represents our conscious interests and intentions. Having a particular destination in mind, the rider directs the elephant toward it. But because the rider weighs less than 1 percent of the elephant's body mass, the rider must lead the animal with clear and precise instructions. In a company context, personal interests are the simple and unambiguous objectives you set for the community you seek to influence. Change Agents who define these objectives crisply and compellingly are the ones who succeed.

The elephant represents the immensity of our sub-rational influences. These influences are largely social in nature, reflecting our desire to belong in a community. They are objectively more powerful than our rational interests, and it's not simply a matter of taming these influences but rather channeling them in the most productive way. In a company context, social influences represent the disproportionately powerful voices that set the pace and tone for the organization. Change Agents actively seek out such voices to recruit them on behalf of their cause.

Finally, the path represents the landscape that determines the passage of the elephant and rider. Tweaks to those surroundings can profoundly influence the journey and destination. In a company context, these structural surroundings come in many forms. They are part of the employee's everyday scenery, as it were. That could include a specific software environment, a recurring meeting, or performance indicators that influence priorities and decision-making day-to-day and week-to-week. Change Agents identify the most salient structural surroundings and consider how to establish a surrogate presence within them.

For the Change Agent, these three things are—I'm afraid the pun is unavoidable—the elephant in the room. They are summarized below in Figure 7.1:

Figure 7.1

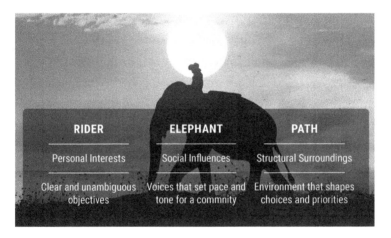

Communicating these concepts is easiest through a story. I have a specific sale in mind, and I'll return to it as I elaborate on each of the above elements. This sale began with a high degree of pessimism and doubt. I was working with a large conglomerate in the manufacturing industry. The company had a complex hierarchy and a highly conservative decision-making process. Our team had been working with this customer for many months, and my manager was growing increasingly anxious about the fact that our main point of contact was an individual contributor who was several layers beneath the executives who would ultimately approve the sale, assuming it ever happened. Ideally, our champion would have been someone more senior. Our fiscal year-end was rapidly approaching, and there was a growing urgency to move things along.

When pushed on the matter, I made the case that this junior employee was actually more influential than his title suggested. I saw how motivated he was to make a name for himself, and how much senior leaders respected him. There was also a nuance to their respect that couldn't be ignored: This was a fast-changing industry, and gray-haired leaders in such a traditional firm seemed to be increasingly open to guidance from junior employees. These lower-ranked employees were considered more up-to-speed on emerging technologies, and often more attuned to organizational sentiment. Our sales team played the role of an outsourced support crew to our junior contact, supplying him with the analysis and storyline he needed to impress his internal stakeholders. In the end, his recommendation was one of the deciding factors in getting our deal across the line. I'll talk about why in a moment.

Looking back, I can see this deal exposed some key principles for the modern sales professional. We now live in a world in which the so-called "wierarchy" (distributed authority) is as important as the hierarchy (top-down authority). Change is happening so quickly that many company leaders maximize organizational responsiveness by relying on "sensing" signals from all levels of the company hierarchy, as was touched upon briefly in the chapter on OKRs. It also means that change is pervasive and continuous, not staggered and discrete as it once was. In the words of futurist Kevin Kelly, we are transitioning to the "third age of computation" in which the "prime units are flows and streams."[1] Everything seems to be in a constant and inexorable state of flux.

In this context, change must be seen as a constant, and rank should no longer be regarded as the primary currency. Rank certainly remains an important variable, but it has declined in value as a natural consequence of our fast and fully connected world. Successful companies today rely on change leaders who can lead with conviction, regardless of title. In this context, sales professionals have an important role to play because they can support internal advocates who drive the change process.

As with Strategy, this requires a different mindset. It requires seeing oneself as an active advisor to the client, not as an order-taker. To make such a mindset shift, sales professionals need a model for the art and science of change leadership. They need a practical framework that helps them skillfully direct the company conversation. As mentioned, the first order of business is to uncover the existing energy source. With this information the Change Agent can then identify the personal, social, and structural levers to make an impact. Returning to the manufacturing company sale as a touchstone, let's talk about how this happens.

CHAPTER 8

What Are Their Personal Interests?

The primary responsibility of a Change Agent is to understand and articulate the dominant motivation of the people you are hoping to change. Typically, these people are the end-users of your product or service. You should be looking to harness the energy behind their pre-existing commitments, in much the same way a surfer uses the energy of a wave. In re-redirecting that energy, you essentially have two options: (1) You can offer a new insight that prompts people to behave differently; or (2) You can provide new information to support a decision they have already made. By far the most efficient path is the second, because there is less friction involved. This is best illustrated through an example from the book *Switch*.

With growing public concerns about health and nutrition in the 1980s, researchers were investigating ways to get people to adopt a healthier diet. However, simply saying "eat healthier" wasn't going to persuade most people. "Eat healthier" was the dominant motivation, but that motivation required precise directions to be useful. People needed crystal clear guidance on what foods they should start and stop eating to improve their health.

The researchers zeroed in on the fact that Americans were already milk drinkers after a successful nationwide campaign to promote the benefits of calcium. Yet the fact that many Americans drank milk was a mixed blessing. Increased milk consumption was providing more calcium, but milk had also become the largest source of saturated fat in the average American's diet. The challenge, then, was to get people to choose 1 percent milk over the full-cream option to which they defaulted on their weekly grocery run.

The researchers' strategy was to take the second route described above: They provided new information to support a decision that people had already made (to drink milk). The new information drew a sharp contrast between full-cream and low-fat milk, explaining in simple terms that 1 percent provided all the benefits of full-cream milk but with significantly fewer health risks. (We'll return to the power of contrast in Part III.) The advertising campaign depicted the perils of full-cream milk in a highly visual way, showing that a single glass had the same amount of saturated fat as five strips of bacon. The goal was to maximize the perceived disparity between low-fat and full-cream milk at the time of purchase, making the switch to low-fat as easy as possible. Following a two-week intervention period, the market share for low-fat milk within the test area doubled over six months.

These principles—channeling the pre-existing energy, making your change request as small and specific as possible—were both at play with the multinational manufacturing company discussed at the beginning of this section. In that case, there had been a company-wide mandate to drive "digital transformation" through various initiatives. These were the equivalent of a prior motivation to "eat healthier." Just as in the milk campaign, we compared our solution to another option that had been considered the incumbent choice. But we isolated the variables to show that while both delivered general benefits, risks would be avoided by choosing our solution over the alternative. Specifically, we pressed our client for details on the competencies they were looking to build in a "digital employee of the future," which was a central part of their change agenda. By working with them to specify these attributes, we could clearly link our solution to the desirable behaviors in this new employee archetype. Equally, we could illustrate how the competition fell short, positioning ourselves as the "healthier" alternative.

In short, we were not looking to create new client motivations but to align ourselves with those that preceded our involvement. Returning to the chemistry analogy, we were attempting to lower barriers to catalysis. We found the key source of energy—digital transformation through the development of new employee competencies—and introduced simple elements to feed that energy. The client was at the grocery store, ready to buy milk, and we ultimately guided them to the low-fat option.

This story highlights one of the key aspects of a Change Agent mindset. Change Agents are perpetually on the lookout for areas of leverage. They attempt to reduce the daunting complexity of company culture to micro decision points with knock-on effects. They find the minimum effective dose that can impact the greatest number of people. Company culture is notoriously unwieldy. It's profoundly difficult for internal leaders to change an organization, let alone outsider teams. The Change Agent must find the most efficient source of traction.

When it comes to personal interests, this usually means engineering an alignment between the target population and the agenda of your key point of contact. For the manufacturing client, most of the sales team (our target population) had good reason to pay attention to digital transformation because the executive team was giving it a lot of airplay. The junior contact was personally committed to this theme because he believed his expertise was valuable and would potentially advance his career. The alignment across leadership interests, our advocate's interests, and the sales team's interests created a potent source of leverage. Let's now look at another potential lever: the social dimension.

CHAPTER 9

Who Are the
Key Influencers?

If you haven't seen the famous 1962 "elevator episode" from *Candid Camera*, illustrating the role of social influences, it's worth a quick look.[1] The *Candid Camera* team sets out to test the power of conformity pressures, with the help of a team of actors. They install hidden cameras to monitor the elevators on several floors of an office building. The actors are instructed to enter the elevator and face the rear wall, not the doors. One of their victims is a gentleman who stands alone at the back of the elevator as the actors begin to surround him. He sees a steady stream of strangers pouring in, and he looks increasingly bewildered as he notes their consistent tendency to face the "wrong" direction. His expression makes it clear that he's struggling with whether to join the crowd or preserve his individuality. The actors staunchly maintain their facade, staring solemnly at the back wall, some of them just inches away from the subject's face. Eventually, little by little, he starts to turn around while pretending to consult his watch, as if this gesture makes his concession to the crowd less noticeable.

The scene illustrates a core truth of human nature. As change experts Grenny and others have definitively stated, "No source of influence is more powerful and accessible than the persuasive power of the people who make up your social networks."[2] Social influences are especially strong today because of the velocity of change we all feel and observe. In times of heightened uncertainty, our natural tendency is to look to others for cues on what to do next. But there are two sides to this coin. The growing pressure to change also creates a powerful countercurrent because of the pervasive "present bias" discussed earlier. Our natural attachment to the status quo prompts many people to seek out respectable peers who can justify a collective resistance to change. (If *they* think it's a waste of time, why should *I* pay any attention, given everything else going on?) Thus, in today's fast-paced business environment, the role of the Change Agent is especially significant.

In *To Sell Is Human*, bestselling author Dan Pink underscores the importance of perspective-taking in sales—empathizing with people and understanding their relationships and connections to others. He called this ability "social cartography," or the capacity to size up a situation and, in one's mind, draw a map of how people are related. Network theory also teaches us that there are "sociometric stars," people who have a disproportionate influence within any organization, shrinking the social world for those around them.[3] Change Agents make a point of mapping the social territory and identifying the sociometric stars who have such outsized influence.

Let's look at some cardinal principles for those who seek to do this. Dr. Everett Rogers is regarded as the world's foremost authority on social support.[4] Many of his initial findings came out of an attempt to persuade farmers in Iowa to adopt a new strain of corn that was objectively superior to the conventional variety these farmers had been using. In terms of yield and resistance to disease, there was simply no rational argument against using the new strain. At first, however, there was no uptake among the farmers because Dr. Rogers lacked credibility with them. From their perspective, his university credentials and brilliant reputation in the academy were meaningless, if not disqualifying. He was perceived as an outsider.

Then Dr. Rogers set out to recruit a potential influencer within the farming community. He found someone who was clearly disposed to unorthodox thinking. This farmer was unabashedly eccentric, typically seen in Bermuda shorts and driving a Cadillac. He was the quintessential innovator. Yet again, however, the farmers were unmoved by this man's endorsement. From their perspective, he was peculiar and unrelatable.

Dr. Rogers was fascinated by the farmers' resistance to change, and over years of subsequent studies he confirmed that what he had experienced was no anomaly. Three things stood out from his body of research. First, the intrinsic merit of an idea has no predictive value for its adoption. "What predicted whether an innovation was widely accepted or not was whether a specific group of people embraced it. Period."[5] Second, and contrary to expectations, "innovators" like the guy in Bermuda shorts are not the most influential. If anything, they should be avoided, rather than courted, by the Change Agent. Third, the true influencers are those who are open to new ideas *and* are both socially connected and respected. These are the "sociometric stars" of network theory. Most people simply won't embrace change until these opinion leaders have done so first.

As I reflected on our team's experience with the multi-national manufacturing company, it's clear that the sale would not have happened without the support of certain people. First and foremost, the client had recently hired a new senior leader to "shake up" the business. Being younger and female, she looked very different from the typical executive. But she quickly became a trusted voice internally, someone who brought a valuable external perspective and carried great influence in her recommendations. Much of the energy around digital transformation, including specific initiatives, was traceable to her. We therefore made it a priority to get time with this leader, and to clearly explain how we could accelerate her change agenda.

There was a second group of highly influential people whose endorsement became critical. Our team did a quick exercise to identify potential influencers, using commercial impact as a guide. Based on publicly available information, we found a clear example of the 80/20 principle.[6] The client's annual report indicated that a small percentage of the team—the roughly 10 percent who managed "global strategic accounts"—were responsible for about 90 percent of revenues. It was clear that this team would have a considerable impact on peer decisions. So we spent time asking several of our client contacts who were the most respected and connected people within this group. We compared the lists of names we were given, and we noted which people came up most often. These were the individuals on whom we concentrated our efforts, offering them a white glove treatment and ensuring we did everything it took to make them champions of the program.

Our traction with the senior executive and the global strategic accounts group was the decisive element of this sale. These stakeholders were also mutually reinforcing sources of influence. We increased the executive's engagement by sharing valuable testimonials from the front lines, helping her stay in tune with the sentiments on the shop floor. From the team's perspective, we raised their profile at the C-suite, highlighting their distinct contribution to the corporate change agenda. All the spadework we did to understand organizational dynamics made it much easier for us to help these stakeholders advance their agenda. Relative to the total number of people affected by this sale, we worked with a modest contingent. But without the support of that contingent, this sale would have been a non-starter.

Here again is the principle of leverage at work. The essential mandate for the Change Agent is to narrow one's focus. Companies are hugely complicated ecosystems, and it's easy to be immobilized by the magnitude of all the variables at play. The mindset of a Change Agent is to seek out and select the few birds that influence the overall flight pattern. Sociometric stars are analogous to those birds. Even slight modifications to their course will have immediate and far-reaching implications for the rest of the flock, because social influences, like the right chemical components, can be deeply catalytic.

There is a third dimension that requires a narrowing of your focus, and those are the structural surroundings we'll explore next.

CHAPTER 10

What Is the Context That Counts?

The more I read about controlled studies designed by social scientists, the more I sense these folks are a roguish lot. Consider this example: In the mid-1970s, a team of psychologists devised an unusual set of conditions to test the hypothesis that people's perception of a situation could be determined by their physiological state, which itself could be influenced by environmental factors. For their test population they chose a crowd of tourists who were passing over a high suspension bridge in a beautiful provincial park in British Columbia, Canada.[1] They then divided this population into two groups: those who had just walked across the bridge, and those who had walked across but had time to allow their slightly elevated heart rate and accelerated breathing to stabilize. A researcher approached people from each of these groups and asked if they would agree to complete a survey about the effects of beautiful scenery on people's creativity. Importantly, the researcher was a woman, and she only chose men as her test subjects. For each man who responded to the survey, the woman thanked him and left her phone number in case there were any follow-up questions about the experiment.

Now, which of these groups do you think was more likely to call the woman back? By a substantial margin— 65 percent versus 30 percent—it was the group of men who had just walked across the suspension bridge. Can you guess why? The researchers speculated it was because these subjects mistook their elevated heart rate and rapid breathing for signs of romantic interest. They called this "misattribution of arousal." But, of course, the subjects' physiology had been engineered by the researchers. The study became a well-known illustration of how circumstantial factors can profoundly influence our perception of reality. What we do follows how we feel, and how we feel is often the result of an emotional cascade that is subconsciously triggered by our surroundings.

Change Agents are highly conscious of how people's perceptions are significantly related to context, whether this takes the form of an everyday software environment or the design of a meeting. In the case of our sale with the multinational manufacturing firm, we made careful use of such variables. First, as we piloted our solution with the target users, we created a custom tag in the CRM system, so that those users had a visual cue to remind them of our solution each time they entered the system. Further, with the help of these tags, we set up tracking mechanisms to give team leaders visibility into user activity. This provided an additional incentive for users to take action within the CRM system, because they knew their activities were being closely monitored.

There was another reason why working within the CRM was so important. The client had recently made a sizable investment in a new CRM platform, and they had taken a go-hard-or-go-home approach. The executive sponsor of their CRM investment had reasoned that, if the company was going to undertake such a substantial technology change, they should fully commit to doing so. He had therefore chosen the gold-plated instance of this CRM, with every conceivable function and feature included. Here, again, was another example of how important it is to find a pre-existing energy source and look for ways to feed it. As the sponsor of such a substantial investment, this executive was highly motivated to ensure it delivered on its promise. Naturally, he felt that anything we could do to increase the team's use of CRM would advance his own agenda.

Our team also put extraordinary preparation into shaping the context of a meeting that had a significant impact on the sales cycle. We learned that our client's executive team was going to be attending a week-long offsite training session. We felt that our solution was relevant to their agenda because it supported some of their priorities around digital transformation. But getting a place on the agenda proved challenging, with the demand for executive attention far exceeding calendar supply. We used our junior sponsor to seed the idea of a 30-minute video call in which we could share an industry point of view that tied into the broader training theme for that day. After several days or jockeying for one of the few spots remaining, we finally secured a place on the calendar.

That meeting proved to be critical. We learned that all the executives would be sitting around a conference table and watching the same screen. We would have their combined attention, and our team's voice would literally fill the room. We prepared assiduously for this meeting, shaping the materials to make the message bigger and bolder than our product alone. When the executives eventually received this message, it was a unifying moment for them. As they sat together, nodding in agreement and processing the key themes, they collectively experienced the potential power of our partnership. One of the executives was prompted to say something along the lines of "Let's do this. We have the money, and there's no reason to delay."

Our deliberate use of structural surroundings made it easier for end-users to remember a solution that hadn't yet become natural to them. We increased their engagement by setting explicit measurement targets, which had the enthusiastic support of a senior sponsor whose vested interests we were helping to advance. Our integration with an executive meeting agenda also gave us a powerful context to present our sales thesis. These were crucial elements to increase awareness and promote the most thoughtful use of our solution, leading to a critical mass of champions at all levels of the company hierarchy. Structural surroundings were an essential building block in our case to the buying committee.

Just as we concluded the Strategy section, let's now look at a story of how a top-performing sales professional made impressive use of these change levers. You'll see evidence of how she applied the personal-social-structural framework, but also went slightly deeper in each of those realms.

CHAPTER 11

The Change Agent
in Action

Andrea was a Senior Account Manager responsible for her company's commercial relationship with a large telecom company. This client was already using one of her firm's software solutions, but only for a specific team. Things were going well with those users, but they were a small portion of the potential user community across the company. Andrea needed to find a way to extend the benefits of this program.

There was a reason why the program had been limited in scope to date. This was a highly risk-averse organization, and it had decided that it would only provide the software solution to those who had asked for it. Company leaders felt much the same as our "customer hero" at the beginning of this section. They were concerned that those on the front lines were already oversubscribed, and they were reluctant to add to the team's workload in the absence of clear and compelling user demand. Andrea's challenge was to change the internal conversation, making the case for an all-in over an opt-in approach. She felt like a tugboat attempting to rotate an ocean liner.

Andrea took a systematic change-leadership approach, slowly but surely redirecting the ship so that it could leave the harbor and hit the high seas. She used the three pillars above—personal, social, and structural considerations—to frame her approach, but within each area she distinguished between *motivation* and *ability* to focus her change efforts.

When it came to **personal interests**, she asked, *What will maximize their engagement?* (motivation) and *How can I minimize complexity?* (ability).

For motivation, she knew that her client's executive team had launched a company-wide initiative to rebrand their competitive positioning. This initiative was regularly discussed at the company all-hands meetings, and it was reinforced through front-line management reminders. There was widespread agreement that the new strategy was too important to fail. There had been public commitments to shareholders, and its executive champions would lose face if the transformation program ran aground. Andrea explicitly framed the goal of her program to support a key element of this new enterprise strategy, ensuring that she aligned with the pre-existing energy and focus.

For ability, she felt that her software solution had many different features that could help the team. The temptation was to offer the full extent of its game-changing potential, checking as many boxes as possible. But she sensed that, given overwhelming demands on people's time, they would ignore most of this information. She needed to focus on one or two specific benefits that would bring disproportionate value to the end-user teams. So, with reference to the client's new go-to-market initiative, she highlighted a single feature that would give the team a leg up in evolving their competitive position.

When it came to **social influences**, she asked, *How can we enlist influencers?* (motivation) and *How can we enable collaboration?* (ability).

For motivation, Andrea worked with her champion to understand which leaders were most respected as innovators across the company. She found evidence of how they had already been successful in driving change, and she referred to these successes in requesting time on their calendars. She mentioned that their peers had nominated them as potential champions of a pilot initiative to test whether a software solution could advance the company's new strategic agenda. These innovators agreed to take part in the pilot, earning Andrea the right to engage their teams.

To increase motivation with one champion in particular, Andrea determined how she could help with career advancement. This champion worked in the marketing organization and was the internal point of contact for several platforms that were dedicated to increasing customer engagement. But this person lacked concrete evidence to prove the ROI for these investments. By including the champion in the pilot program, Andrea strengthened this person's internal credibility with stronger data and success stories to highlight some of her professional wins. That made the marketing lead a vocal advocate in short order.

For ability, Andrea was aware that identifying strong influencers was just the first step. People would be motivated to follow the lead of these individuals, but they would need support mechanisms to do so. Andrea highlighted the power of her firm's solution to increase collaboration across the business. She felt it would enhance people's ability to do so if they had a concrete example to follow. Noticing how her social influencers were collaborating effectively, she took what they had done as a basis for a reusable template. In sharing this template, she empowered others to replicate what was known to have worked with their well-respected peers, reducing the effort required to try a different approach

When it came to **structural surroundings**, Andrea asked, *How can we incentivize behavior?* (motivation) and *How can we shape context?* (ability).

For motivation, she took stock of where people were spending most of their time. Her target audience was the sales team, and she realized they held monthly deal reviews to share successes and support peers. Attendees were motivated to pay attention and learn from others. It was the perfect environment to be embedded within. Since Andrea's current team of users already participated in this forum, she thought it would be a good opportunity for them to highlight one or two wins on a regular basis. She offered to help her sponsor by preparing some "micro lessons" for each deal review session. She suggested this would be of mutual benefit: He would add more value to the meeting, and her program would gain more visibility.

For ability, Andrea also used the structural environment to stay top of mind. In addition to one-off training sessions, she and her team put together a series of short videos that highlighted tips and tricks. These videos were released at regular intervals and, with the help of her sponsor, added to the training site that was a standard place for the sales team to visit. Andrea's supplementary materials became an important part of their "surround sound" experience of her program.

After pushing these change initiatives over several months, Andrea's ring-fenced program had achieved a high level of visibility at the leadership level. When it came time to renew her existing footprint, it was a straightforward decision to shift from "opt-in" to "all-in."

As Andrea reflected on the experience, she was struck by a couple of things. First, the three pillars of the change program were mutually reinforcing—for example, a clear understanding of personal interests had helped recruit strong social influencers, and having strong social influencers had further stoked the flames of personal interest. This underscored the fact that the pillars were not sequential but overlapping considerations. Second, the power of these levers increased as more of them were used. Andrea later learned that this was consistent with what academic studies had rigorously demonstrated. An MIT experiment involving more than a thousand managers, as well as a thousand individuals who were attempting to implement significant change in their lives, tested the degree to which six potential levers—personal, social, and structural levers, each of them broken into motivation and ability—could impact the desired change. The study revealed a tenfold increase in change effectiveness when four or more of the six dimensions were engaged.[1] Although Andrea had initially felt overwhelmed by the challenge of influencing such a large organization, she now understood that a systematic focus on these change elements can spark an impressive "chemical transformation."

There was one final lesson that Andrea took from the experience. She realized that decision-makers have a different standard of proof in the later stages of a sales cycle. In the earlier phases, they are most interested in evaluating whether a new product or service warrants their attention. In the later stages, as they move to a decision on whether to invest, they are looking for proof that the solution will deliver on its promise, particularly with software and services. In short, they are looking for experiential value. This means they rely heavily on proxy evidence, often in the form of pilot results. Equally, though, they look for confirmation that the salesperson can effectively summon their firm's capabilities to support the client. That's what Andrea had demonstrated so convincingly. She had given them an indicative sense of what the implementation of her solution would feel like. Here, too, she confirmed the results of a classic study that found executives' most important criterion in evaluating salespeople is the ability to marshal their firm's resources.[2]

While Strategist skills are most important in the early stages of the sales cycle, where it is important to align with the company agenda, Change Agent skills become increasingly powerful in the later stages, and especially when the client relies on experiential value to make an investment decision. Andrea's story shows how the Change Agent can diminish the client's present bias by mitigating the potential for future risks. Through a parallel focus on the client organization's personal, social, and structural dimensions, she made the value of her solution tangible for them, creating the right conditions to support a new direction.

Andrea's story further illustrates the importance of psychology in sales. In many respects, selling to large organizations is analogous to guerilla warfare. Sales teams can feel like a small band of brothers and sisters who are confronting a massive, and apparently overwhelming, military force. Their challenge is to make themselves seem more significant than their raw numbers might suggest. Under such conditions, the mindset of the Change Agent is remarkably similar to that of a guerrilla combatant. Success depends on the ability to achieve company-wide recognition with localized actions, leading decision-makers to feel that your team is omnipresent. We've talked about how to use personal, social, and structural levers within the organization to achieve this effect, but now let's go deeper on the interpersonal level. Let's look at the principles that govern human perception, helping you to sharpen your message design.

TAKEAWAYS FOR THE CHANGE AGENT

The Change Agent mindset prioritizes factors that influence human behavior in large organizations. Here are the key points:

- Change is analogous to "catalysis" in chemistry: You let it happen by removing barriers and introducing a small number of elements to accelerate the process of transformation.
- The most significant barrier to overcome is the customer's "present bias."
- The client's aversion to change is best attributed to circumstantial variables, and it is the responsibility of the Change Agent to proactively work with those variables.
- A Change Agent asks, *Where is the energy for change coming from?* and *How can I feed that energy?*
- The Change Agent then focuses on three levers: personal interests, social influences, and structural surroundings. Within each of those domains, they distinguish between what will drive people (motivation) and what will help them succeed (ability).
- The following table outlines key goals, questions, and actions to consider:

Table 1

	GOAL	QUESTIONS	ACTIONS
PERSONAL INTERESTS	Maximize Engagement	• What do end users care about? • What initiatives command their attention?	1. Define the 'why' for end users.
	Minimize Complexity	• What are 1–3 critical new skills for the end users? • How can we support the development of these skills with our product/service?	2. Prioritize key skills.
SOCIAL INFLUENCERS	Enlist Influencers	• Which leaders could reinforce the importance of the program? • Which peers could set an example for others?	3. Nominate strongest influencers.
	Enable Collaboration	• What can we templatize or standardize to make things easier? • What else could facilitate collaboration within the community?	4. Create collaboration mechanisms.
STRUCTURAL SURROUNDINGS	Incentivize Behavior	• Are there existing metrics to support our priorities? • Are there new metrics that could increase motivation?	5. Leverage key performance metrics.
	Shape Context	• Can we create a stronger presence in the software environment? • Can we integrate with recurring training, meetings, and learning sessions?	6. Integrate with meetings, trainings, and technologies.

PART III: BECOMING A DECISION ARCHITECT

"A change in perspective is worth 80 IQ points."

—ALAN KAY

CHAPTER 12

What's Most Important? Why Will They Care?

My family and I once took a vacation in Europe, where we spent three weeks eating too much and doing almost nothing active. It was sublime. On the way back home, we stopped at a trendy café in Athens. I looked at the menu, and my eyes were immediately drawn to the smoothie section. It had all sorts of enticing concoctions, including a "Dieter's Special" for burning fat, an "Anti-Aging Elixir" for recovering youth, and a "Love Potion" for rejuvenating libido. Predictably, the prices were exorbitant. I pondered these ridiculous health promises with contempt. "Do they really think I'm an idiot?" I said aloud. "Do they actually believe that I would buy one of these things, thinking that it would deliver the benefits they claim? Is *anyone* that gullible?" Our family had a good chuckle at the absurdity of the idea.

But when the waiter took our order, I simply couldn't resist. I had spent the last three weeks defying all my usual protocols on exercise and food consumption. In this moment, I wanted to make a renewed commitment to my health. So, with a bashful look at my wife and kids, I ordered the "Dieter's Special," triggering a barrage of ridicule from my daughters after the waiter had left our table. I distinctly recall the sensation as I made the order. On the one hand, I knew perfectly well that it made no sense logically. Clearly the drink itself would do nothing to burn fat. On the other hand, I simply couldn't deny that it made me feel good to order it. I wanted to *feel* that I was doing the right thing for my body. It was this feeling that drove me to act.

I often look back on that moment as a gleaming portal into human psychology. We've all justified our concession to irrationality on many occasions. On some level we understand that none of us—even corporate clients— makes buying decisions according to rational criteria. We're just too vulnerable to the same impulses that sabotaged my evaluation of the smoothie menu. Indeed, a general rule of thumb is that the bigger and more complex the decision, the more susceptible we are to these sub-rational forces. When buying a stapler, for example, you can legitimately claim immunity. Under those specific conditions, rationality will likely prevail. Choosing a spouse, on the other hand, is the furthest thing from a rational deliberation.

Human irrationality gets a lot of coverage these days. There has been an explosion of interest in behavioral economics due to the profound influence of works by Daniel Kahneman, Richard Thaler, Dan Ariely, and others. This section is going to be a selective distillation of this literature, but with a view to what's most relevant to those who sell to enterprise buyers. You will have noticed that I've been hinting at this psychological dimension in the previous sections, which went into the buyer's frame of mind and the cognitive impact of circumstantial elements. Now we go deeper.

Decision architecture is the art and science of designing the choices from which a decision is made. It is about how we organize information to create the optimal user experience, comparable to the way a web page designer anticipates and directs the journey of each new visitor to a site. The smoothie menu had clearly been designed to elicit an instinctual response. In a sales context, the Decision Architect approaches important client conversations with two questions in mind: *What details are worth emphasizing?* and *How can I get my audience to care about those details?* The principles and examples in this section are designed to support these deliberations.

To begin, I'll discuss three key limitations of human cognition. These fundamentals are important to review because they represent the psychological guardrails within which most sales conversations take place. For each of these limitations, we'll discuss two potential ways to navigate them. The two approaches have been selected from a range of possibilities, but they have proven to be powerful and are a good place to begin building your repertoire. In each case, we'll examine the theory behind the suggested approach, and then move to practical examples drawn from what I've seen play out with clients and colleagues. The goal is to help you work more effectively within these cognitive boundaries, building Decision Architect skills that enhance the power of your message with clients.

This section continues the broader theme of mindset progression. We're cultivating a new way to view yourself and the situation. Top-performing sales professionals see themselves as capable of influencing the few controllable factors in a complex sale. They isolate those factors and prioritize the need to manage them. Top performers are also in tune with many of the less obvious variables at play. Their power of influence stems from a closer reading of situational nuances. I want to help you appreciate some of these nuances so you can approach sales challenges with greater care and precision.

CHAPTER 13

What Constrains Their Perception?

Behavioral economics emerged from the realization that traditional economics was wrong to assume rational agency as the primary basis for human decision-making. The founders of behavioral economics proposed a new framework, one that explicitly acknowledged the bounds of human willpower, rationality, and self-interest.[1] I'm going to use the same framework as a starting point for this section, replacing "willpower" with "attention." The reason for beginning with this framework is that it gets to the heart of the sales challenge. At the most basic psychological level, what are you looking to achieve with corporate buyers and influencers? I would suggest three things: (1) to get them to pay attention to the problem you've identified; (2) to get them to make the correct judgment about that problem; and (3) to prompt them to seek your help in solving the problem. It sounds simple enough in theory, but it's extraordinarily difficult in practice. That's because these bounds of human cognition constrain the client's ability to notice, evaluate, and act upon your recommendations.

BOUNDS OF ATTENTION

The first step in persuasion is to get someone's attention. Until someone is focused on what you have to say, even the greatest pitch will have been in vain. Bounds of attention are the mortal enemy of the sales professional because of the grinding logic of our Information Age. The nature of information is that it's inherently limitless. There is always more to know and build upon in the knowledge economy. Further, the modern communication system is effectively infinite. As Internet nodes continue to multiply, the volume of information inexorably compounds. This is the baseline reality that explains why each of us feels that things are only getting busier. It is also why we continually have the sense that people aren't giving us their full attention in internal and external meetings. What are the practical ramifications for a sales professional?

Brains are reductionist.

The single biggest impediment to effective communication is message overreach. In other words, the communicator tries to convey too much. Tim Pollard's excellent book *The*

Compelling Communicator spells this out most brilliantly. He reminds us that the brain processes new information with "working memory," and he uses a powerful analogy to illustrate the limits of our working memory capacity.[2] Imagine that the total processing power of your brain is roughly equivalent to the US economy, which today (2022) is around 23 trillion dollars. What would you say is the total processing power, in dollars, that your brain allocates to working memory? Apparently, it's about three dollars.

Our brains have no choice but to triage the barrage of inbound messaging. We write off most of it as irrelevant, and radically simplify the rest. Stand-out communicators boil things down to simple, memorable themes because these have the highest chance of breaking the bounds of attention.

Fitting in is failing.

Earlier on, I mentioned marketing guru Seth Godin. One of his books, *Purple Cow*, argues that fitting in is a failing when it comes to our crowded marketplace. Not standing out is the same as being invisible. Those who sell to busy people—and, again, everyone is busy—need to challenge themselves and ask, "How can we be more memorable? How can we frame things in a way that sticks in people's minds?" Cognitive scientist Daniel Willingham once observed that "memory is the residue of thought"—things that leave durable fragments behind are more likely to be recalled later on. Generally, the most memorable things are some combination of unexpected, visual, and emotional elements. One of my colleagues achieves this effect with handwritten notes he periodically sends to clients. Such a gesture checks all three boxes: No one expects it in the age of email; personal handwriting is more visually distinctive; and the act itself shows a deeper level of human warmth.

To some extent the best way to stand out will always be a moving target. What separates you from others today may become annoyingly commonplace by tomorrow. (Video prospecting springs to mind as an example.) You should be attuned to the latest trends, but never a thoughtless subscriber to them.

Influence is transitory.

Despite these headwinds, the situation is not as bad as it sounds. You have potent levers to work with once you get to a face-to-face or virtual interaction. It's surprisingly easy to direct someone's attention. Consider this trivial example: I can tell you to think about the sensation in your left arm right now. Up until you read that sentence, you probably weren't thinking about your left arm at all. Simply by calling attention to it I've changed your field of focus. But I'm working with borrowed time. You're already starting to wonder whether you should continue to contemplate the arm or move on to more pressing concerns. If I don't make the most of this window of opportunity, I'm back to where we started.

Think about the implications of this example: Despite my lack of formal authority over you as a reader I had the power to shape your perception, if only fleetingly. You have the same capability when interacting with buyers and influencers, even those at the executive level. But while you can proactively redirect their attention, you must make the most of these transitory opportunities. I'll give you a practical example of how to do so in the upcoming explanation of the "Peak-End Rule."

BOUNDS OF RATIONALITY

Assuming you manage to get noticed, it's important to understand the bounds within which information is processed. As shown in the smoothie example, reason and emotion are deeply intertwined. And in more complex decision-making, it's emotion that tends to have the upper hand. "Emotion" is shorthand for the many factors that override logic and rationality, and I'll prioritize three of them below. These help us understand how a client makes judgments about the problem you've presented.

Truth is relative.

We don't need to get into a deep philosophical discussion about how we know what we know. We simply need to acknowledge that the way information is presented profoundly determines what we feel is true. The easiest way to illustrate this point is through well-known visual examples like Figure 13.1:

Figure 13.1 Relative vs. Absolute Perception

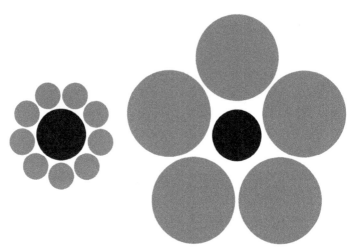

On a rational level, we know that the black circle in the middle is the same size in both pictures. But knowing what's rationally accurate doesn't change what we *feel* is true. We make an inescapable judgment based on a comparison to the adjacent shapes. People's perception of truth is significantly determined by context, and context can be designed to influence that perception. Sellers should be keenly attentive to the points of comparison in what they present to clients. I'll cover this in the upcoming discussion of "The Contrast Effect."

Facts don't matter.

The evidence has been clear for some time that facts are less relevant than we tend to think. Consider the experience of two executives who interviewed a candidate who was formerly the Chief Financial Officer of a mid-sized company.

The executives noted that he had resigned from this position after only a few months, so in separate interviews they asked him why. The candidate's explanation was consistent: strategic disagreement with the CEO. But when the two interviewing executives met to agree on a hiring decision, they had radically different perspectives on the candidate. One had formed a positive impression of him, and she saw his decision to leave as a sign of courage and integrity. The other had come away with a negative impression, and he interpreted the resignation as an example of inflexibility. Here, as in so many other examples, people's interpretation of facts was colored by their pre-existing attitudes.[3] Once such attitudes have been established, people filter information to shore up their prior commitments. Sales professionals must bear this in mind as they think about how to sequence information with clients.

Reasoning is social.

Despite all the bugs and flaws in the human brain, we have managed to survive and thrive as a species—for good and for ill. Perhaps, then, there is a flipside to all these flaws. Perhaps evolution can help us better understand the net positive effects. To me, the most intriguing theory posits a connection between our rationalizing nature and the development of human language some 50,000–150,000 years ago.[4] The theory maintains that human reason emerged primarily to justify ourselves to others in a social setting. This in turn led to increasingly sophisticated language systems, helping us to cooperate more effectively with kith, kin, and ultimately with strangers on a global scale. According to this theory, reason was never designed to apprehend objective truth. It emerged as the handmaiden of our social nature. I find this to be a liberating insight. It puts the bounds of rationality in context, revealing the pragmatic origins of seemingly absurd human traits. It reminds us that the most effective arguments reflect the values and priorities of the group we are working with. The best sales professionals seek out such community values and priorities like an investigative journalist, and then incorporate them in their communications. I'll get into some examples of this in the upcoming discussion of "Naming and Norming."

BOUNDS OF SELF-INTEREST

Let's now assume you've scaled two of the three walls surrounding the client. You've managed to get her attention. You've framed the problem in such a way that she considers it to be important. Your final challenge is to inspire her to act. What is the most reliable way to do so? Unquestionably, there needs to be an element of self-interest. Here are the stark psychological realities we should briefly revisit.

Everyone is a hero.

The tendency to overestimate one's ability and exaggerate one's importance is deeply ingrained in human nature. To provide a sense of how extreme this tendency is, I refer you to a 1997 *US News & World Report* survey, in which

1,000 Americans were asked, "Who do you think is most likely to get to heaven?" Survey respondents were given the names of several public figures, including Mother Teresa, Princess Diana, Bill Clinton, and Michael Jordan. As expected, Mother Teresa did exceptionally well: 79 percent of respondents agreed the gates of heaven would open for her. Princess Diana also received a respectable endorsement of 60 percent, though it was just shy of the great Michael Jordan (65 percent). But there was one clear winner in the survey, and I'll bet you can guess who it was. That's right: each respondent. When asked about themselves, 87 percent of survey respondents said they were likely to get to heaven— fully 10 percentage points higher than a canonized saint.

The same phenomenon plays out in rarefied circles, such as the world of forensic science (using scientific investigations to gather evidence for legal verdicts). Within this highly educated community there is widespread acknowledgment that bias is a problem. In fact, in a survey of 400 professional forensic scientists in 21 countries, 71 percent agreed that "cognitive bias is a cause for concern in the forensic sciences as a whole." However, only 26 percent thought that their "own judgments are influenced by cognitive bias."[5] That's how deeply we tend to believe in our own virtue and capability. This is a key starting point in thinking about how to prompt the client to act. There must be a clear sense in which they are made to feel heroic.

Heroes need reassurance.

The interesting thing about humans is that, although we tend to exaggerate our own importance, our egos are also fragile.

None of us is fully secure in the knowledge that others like and respect us. Doubts begin to leak through the cracks of our confidence. We regularly seek validation to affirm that we are a good and well-respected person. Even when we get that validation, it's never quite enough. The ego always wants more. As you interact with influencers and decision-makers, it's helpful to ask yourself how you can reinforce someone's hero status, even with more senior clients for whom you might assume this would be less important. I'll discuss this further in the upcoming section on "Role Theory."

Self-preservation is primary.

A final dimension to consider is the primacy of self-preservation. Clearly a preservation instinct has been one of the keys to our survival as a species. Human history has rewarded those who took stronger protective measures to stay alive. Mostly, this was a matter of physical survival, but a protective instinct is also at the heart of our egoic life in modern times. This explains the hero complex and the craving for reassurance that was just discussed. Modern professionals, like ancient humans, default to a defensive posture. But they are defending a self-concept, not just a physical body. Anything that threatens an established sense of who we are is something we fight hard against, consciously and unconsciously. That self-protective impulse is also something the seller must constantly be alive to.

We can think of these three bounds of human cognition as lines on the playing field. We can view sales as a game taking place within those bounds. What we want to do now is study some of the maneuvers that have proven to work, based on research in the behavioral sciences. Like an actual sports game, cause and effect are not perfectly predictable in this realm. There are just too many unknowns and unknowable factors involved. But there are still observable patterns, and with a better grasp of these patterns we can develop a bolder mindset as we approach sales conversations. As with the study of sports, we shouldn't aspire to replicate the precise sequence that was once successful. We should instead tease out the principles that prevailed. Examining these principles should expand your perspective on the range of options available, and it should give you ideas to experiment with as you confront your own sales challenges.

CHAPTER 14

How Can You Speak to the Subconscious?

As Daniel Kahneman explained in *Thinking Fast and Slow*, the human brain makes judgments using two systems of thought.[1] "System 1" relies on instinct and intuition. It is unconscious, fast, and associative. "System 2" relies on logic and reason. It is effortful, slow, and methodical. Most of our decisions—reportedly about 95 percent of them—are System 1 decisions because of the sheer amount of information we're processing every day. The busier we get, the more reliant on System 1 we become. Thus, it's not only the case that most of our judgments are made using fast and associative thinking; it's also true that the current pace of change guarantees an even greater reliance on System 1 modes of thought. This has profound implications for the sales professional. It raises the bar for what sellers need to know about interpersonal dynamics. A solid grounding in human psychology is required to secure and direct a client's attention in this noisy world.

Before Daniel Kahneman became a household name, a book called *Influence: The Psychology of Persuasion* by Robert Cialdini was the intellectual harbinger of our current behavioral economics craze. The book was published in 1984 and it has sold more than 3 million copies worldwide, having been translated into 30 languages. It's a classic of business literature, and it remains a must-read for anyone in sales. Cialdini's research revealed that effective persuasion makes use of one or more of seven influence levers. These levers are substitutes for reason. They are shorthand cues that play to our System 1 thinking patterns, sparing us the time and effort required to engage System 2. All of us are routinely exposed to these levers. They have become part of the furniture of our lives. To illustrate, let me walk you through seven things that have happened to me in the last week, each of which brings to life one of Cialdini's principles:

- Yesterday I bought some shaving oil on Amazon. I had no idea which brand to buy, and as I surveyed the seemingly infinite number of options, I was immediately hostile to the idea of having to investigate each one. So, I took the path of least resistance, using the wisdom of crowds as my guide. I chose the one that was reassuringly popular. This was **social proof** in action.

- I go through many books, and this week I added another one to the pile. What tipped my hand was an endorsement from a famous author whose opinion I greatly admire. This was **authority** in action. Instead of sampling the first chapter of the book, as I might have easily done, a thumbs-up from this author was sufficient.

- Earlier today my 13-year-old daughter approached me in a panic. She had been shopping online, and she had found the *perfect dress*. Disconcertingly, the site informed her that there was only one left in stock! This was the emergency that justified her interruption of my conference call. It was a case of **scarcity** in action. That website, like so many others, was playing to the reliable human fear of missing out.

- Over the weekend my wife and I went out to dinner. After paying the bill, I realized that my tip percentage had been slightly higher than usual, and that there were probably subconscious factors at play. I recalled that our waiter had given my wife and me a free shot of grappa just before presenting the bill, ostensibly to thank us for our regular patronage. My larger tip was probably a case of **reciprocity** in action. (Indeed, studies have shown that extra mints to accompany the check materially increase tipping.)[2]

- A couple of days ago I pledged to revive my workout routine at the local gym after receiving a personalized birthday message from one of the trainers.

I appreciated his reaching out, even as I knew the prompt must have been an electronic reminder. I felt positively disposed toward him because he made me feel special. This was a case of **likeability** in action.

- Last night I heard a knock at the front door. I didn't recognize the guy standing on my porch as I peeked through the window. Then, as I opened the door, I noticed he had a clipboard and name tag. Clearly, I was about to be pressed for a donation. He began by saying, "Good evening, sir. I'm so sorry to interrupt. This will be quick. Is it safe to assume you are a kind person?" Naturally, I confirmed I was. He briefly described the purpose of his charity before we came to the moment of truth. I so much wanted to return to the dinner table, but I felt compelled to stay in the conversation because I had just declared that I was "kind." This was a case of **commitment and consistency** in action.

- There was another detail that this young man had picked up on. He noticed I was wearing a South African rugby shirt, and he mentioned how much he loved the city of Cape Town, which he had once visited because his mother was born there. The kid was annoyingly savvy, and I couldn't deny that he increased my sense of connection to him by pointing out this cultural commonality (I was born in Cape Town, too). That was **unity** in action.

These triggers are so pervasive in our society because they have repeatedly proven to be effective. I'm sure you can think of several illustrations in your own life from the last week, if not the last 24 hours.

Let's now look at how these influence levers are used in B2B sales communications. Below is a redacted version of a top performer's prospecting email that stands out to me as a great example of how to strengthen one's messaging with Cialdini's principles. She was reaching out to an executive leader in a new area of the customer's organization. Her company was already working with another team, and she was exploring ways to expand the business relationship. I'll share the email first, and then we'll analyze why it succeeded in getting an immediate response. As you're reading it, try to spot the technique.

> Hi Jeff —
>
> Hello from a fellow SEC alum and your Relationship Manager for _____. Though my Missouri Tigers regularly rank near the very bottom since joining the SEC, we're just happy to be here!
>
> Football aside, I work with more than 600 of your colleagues, helping them create new business opportunities with better market intel. Mike Kirkland recommended I get your perspective on what would be most effective in coaching the current users, and possibly to discuss the use case for your team. Are you open to connecting this week or next, while we still have a few remaining weeks to find more revenue in this fiscal year?

> I also invited Mike to an exclusive peer-to-peer
> roundtable that might interest you, too (details here). The
> session will feature some [Research Company] insights
> and learnings from your peers in other industries on how
> to manage a fully remote team today. The event will be
> capped at 25 to ensure it's a small group discussion, and I
> hope you'll be able to attend!
> Best,
> Jennifer

A lot is happening in this short message. Let's review it from top to bottom and highlight all the influence levers at play.

> Hello from a fellow SEC alum ... though my Missouri
> Tigers regularly rank near the very bottom since joining the
> SEC, we're just happy to be here!

This is a brilliant use of **likeability** and **unity** because of how natural and balanced it feels. First, Jennifer establishes a common identity with the recipient by pointing out that she is part of the same alumni community. She correctly senses that a prospect is more likely to be open to someone who shares the same background. But she doesn't overplay it. In fact, she seems to understand how tenuous this commonality may be. After all, an American college athletic conference is not a particularly exclusive alumni group. So, she immediately shifts to a self-deprecating tone, acknowledging the shortcomings of her team. The reader is naturally sympathetic to someone who calls attention to her misfortunes in such a good-humored way.

> I work with more than 600 of your colleagues …

Jennifer immediately establishes her firm's credibility through **social proof**. The fact that 600 colleagues are already on board is a shorthand way to communicate that another leader has done the due diligence and concluded her solution was worth the investment for a substantial number of people.

> Mike Kirkland recommended I get your perspective …

This line is a savvy combination of **social proof** and **likeability**. Jennifer uses Mike as a reference because she feels that Jeff is likely to defer to the judgment of a senior and well-respected colleague. But embedded in that reference is a claim about Jeff's internal brand. Apparently, his perspective is considered important enough that Jennifer was asked to seek it out. This pulls the likeability lever for Jeff because she has made him feel special.

> … while we still have a few remaining weeks to find more revenues in the fiscal year?

This line invokes potential **scarcity**. Jennifer doesn't know everything that's going on in Jeff's world, but she can confidently predict that one of his key priorities is to close the fiscal year strong. By reminding him that there is a shrinking window in which to do so, she makes him more aware of what he may lose by hesitating to act quickly.

> I also invited Mike to an exclusive peer-to-peer roundtable that might interest you, too … the event will be capped at …

As her note draws to a close, Jennifer pulls the **reciprocity, social proof,** and **scarcity** levers in rapid succession. She invites Jeff to a valuable thought leadership session, encouraging a sense of gratitude in him. She legitimizes the invitation by mentioning that Mike received one as well. Finally, she makes it clear that there will be limited spaces available.

> The session will feature some insights ... and learnings
> from your peers in other industries ...

Jennifer communicates the value of the roundtable discussion with **authority**. She knows it will undercut the appeal of her invitation if the roundtable is perceived to be a self-serving forum. So, she makes it clear that the insights will come from a third party. And, once again, she plays to **social proof** by telling Jeff that he can learn what other companies are doing in the market. Rather than invest hours in his own research, he can simply ask them directly.

Jennifer's email worked so well because it made excellent use of influence levers. She moved impressively within the bounds of attention to maximize the possibility that Jeff would engage her. She also showed the power of a more elevated mindset. Consider at least three forms of objectivity that contributed to the strength of her communication. First, she took a step back and developed a picture of her prospect's identity, identifying alumni connections and potential areas of interest. Second, she thought about his relationship with colleagues and peers, positioning him as an integral part of a broader social context. Finally, she detached from her own ego, humorously disparaging herself in a way that took her sales persona out of the equation. It's a perfect illustration of what a different mindset can accomplish.

Notice, as well, the compounding strength of these influence levers as they coalesce and combine. Her persuasive power seems to build in non-linear fashion with the use and re-use of different techniques. But the excellence on display is also attributable to Jennifer's careful and astute phrasing. One can certainly go too far and overplay the above techniques, making readers feel as if they need a hot shower after pressing "delete." Artfulness matters, and artful execution is only achieved through repeated testing and practice. Mindset sets the stage for a deeper and wider range of skills, and these skills must be refined through continuous contact with reality.

CHAPTER 15

What Creates a Memory?

Imagine you took two trips last year. Both included some old friends from university, but each trip was very different. The first was much shorter. You and your friends flew into the same city for a weekend getaway. There was a welcome dinner on Friday night, a concert on Saturday, and a brunch on Sunday before everyone left. It was a condensed experience, but emotions spiked quickly, and the bonding was deep. The second trip was a more extended and relaxed affair. One of these friends had a family cottage by the lake, and this friend invited everyone to spend two weeks off the grid. The friend made it clear there would be no expectations: you could read a book by the dock, catch up on work, go for walks, or whatever. The important thing was just to be there, and to spend time with people in a way that was natural and spontaneous.

If you were to reflect on these two trips, which would you be more likely to recall as the most enjoyable one? On the face of it, you might be tempted to think the second trip. For one thing, that trip was about five times longer. There was clearly more space to fill with positive memories. It was also less constrained in how you spent the time, allowing for greater freedom and control. But the evidence suggests you would tend to have a more positive recollection of the first trip because of something called the Peak-End Rule.

The origins of this rule once again reveal the mischievous side of the behavioral economics community. A team of researchers set out to establish how memories are formed. These scientists wanted to understand the relationship between real-time sensations and the later recollection of those sensations. They were curious to know whether changing the duration and intensity of an uncomfortable moment would significantly alter the way someone remembered that moment. They gathered around a table to design the test conditions, stroking their chins in quiet contemplation, until one of the researchers said, "I think I have it!" raising his index finger triumphantly. "Why don't we conduct the experiment on patients undergoing colonoscopy treatment?"

The colonoscopy trials—surely a Netflix series begging for release—revealed the principles on display in our thought experiment about the two trips with college friends.[1] The study revealed how our memory of an experience is imperfect and susceptible to bias. It showed that memories are more selective than we tend to assume. In essence, while we think we remember the full experience, we are profoundly influenced by its final moments and by the peak levels of intensity we recall. In this way we reconstruct the past based on "peak" and "end" impressions. You could say that our memory math is essentially the average of the best and worst moments, as well as the final moment, of any experience. We are largely indifferent to the duration of the experience. The memory math formula looks something like Figure 15.1, below:

Figure 15.1

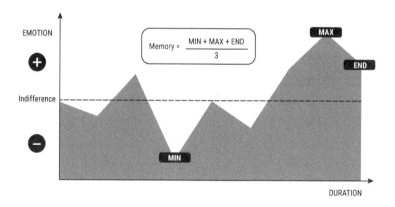

$$\text{Memory} = \frac{\text{MIN} + \text{MAX} + \text{END}}{3}$$

This also implies there is a significant difference between our "experiencing self" and our "remembering self." Experience is the real-time perception of what is giving us pleasure or pain. Memory is another instance of the brain's tendency to simplify the complex, because memory involves radically summarizing the past. Instead of recalling every prior sensation, we single out key moments and combine them with the last thing we can remember. Primacy and recency are the dominant reference points.

You may well be wondering how this discussion of concerts, cottages, and colonoscopies applies to the B2B sales process. Here's how: Selling into any large organization involves a long series of conversations. Conversational proficiency is therefore a fundamental skill for a sales professional. The best sellers are those who make every interaction count, ensuring there is an optimal "peak" and "end" to each meeting. The chain of client conversations is like a series of compound interest earnings: Each installment may not seem significant, but they add up to outsized returns over time. The most skillful salespeople I've come across know how to manage their conversations in a focused and deliberate way, building emotional momentum from one meeting to the next.

Once again, such an approach is rooted in a more detached mindset. Rather than seeing each conversation as an end itself, the best sellers take a more objective view, designing the meeting agenda and approach to create a feeling of continuity. The interaction becomes a single frame in the film reel of their deal progression. It is an opportunity to make the audience feel as though they are involved in the unfolding of a story, not simply taking part in a one-off dialogue. It is a chance to highlight the feats of the past and preview the triumphs of the future.

Here's an example. My team and I once kicked off a pilot program with a large global software company. We had brought several senior executives to the table because they were critical sponsors of the initiative. But it was going to be a challenge to keep them engaged. For one thing, these were extremely busy leaders, and they would almost certainly perceive the pilot as less important than other things they had on the go. For another, this was a virtual meeting, and there is always a powerful temptation for executives to multitask when they enjoy the cover of an inconspicuous avatar on a Zoom panel.

I watched a colleague manage these circumstances beautifully. He started off by politely asking if everyone could participate by video: "I completely understand if video isn't possible today, but if you're able to switch on your camera we'd love to see you," he said. This broke the ice, and all the execs switched to video mode. My colleague got straight to the point by laying out a crisp agenda, clarifying the structure and objectives for the next 30 minutes. But then he did something that noticeably loosened up the executive audience. For the "introductions" part of the agenda, he asked each of them to share something that was not on their LinkedIn profile. Many of the executives took an extra minute to describe some aspect of their personal lives that was meaningful. These disclosures created a warmer human connection before we got into the rest of the agenda. A "peak" was quickly taking shape.

As we approached the end of the call, my colleague transitioned to the last agenda item. He wanted to leave the executives with a sense of how things were going so far. To paint a picture for them, he had assembled a series of vignettes from the field, pulling together names and photos of recognizable team members. He shared quotes from these team members, using their testimonials to explain how our solution had contributed to overcoming problems known to be important to these executives. You could see the effect this evidence had on them. They nodded their heads vigorously as they heard accounts of these early wins from the field. The "end" was also proving to be strong as well. These executives were mentally preparing for their next call, and they were looking for cues to sign off from the meeting. Psychologically, they were primed for an "end" impression to carry away with them. My colleague gave them something positive, personal, and concrete. He ended the call on an emotional high note, and they were visibly upbeat as they signed off.

That conversation teed up a long line of follow-up conversations as we proved out the hypothesis of this pilot. Importantly, the executives who took part in this initial discussion stayed engaged. My colleague made them feel connected to the program, and this initial discussion motivated them to stay on top of program developments. He had deftly maneuvered within the bounds of attention, making full use of the limited time he had available. Conversational proficiency involves many skills, and a vital element is knowing how to maximize positive emotions—not just in the moment, but over repeated interactions.

To manage the bounds of attention, Decision Architects work from a higher plane when engaging their prospects and clients. They start with human universals in thinking about how to craft their message, making careful and deliberate—but not excessive—use of influence levers. They take the long view in their approach to conversations, striving for a steady buildup in momentum. Finally, they prioritize the perspective of the client, downplaying their ego and shrinking their sales persona.

CHAPTER 16

Compared to What?

Let's now consider two ways of managing the bounds of rationality. Imagine you lost your phone and need to replace it in short order. I then show up at your front door as a representative from your local cell service provider. (If only their customer support teams were this good!) I show you a newer model of whatever phone you had been using, and I describe its many features and functions. Then I ask whether you wish to buy the new model I've shown. What would be your response? Almost certainly you would say, "Well, are there any other options I can look at before making a decision?" Why is that such a predictable reaction? Because it's incredibly difficult for us to decide in the absence of contrast. We just don't judge things in isolation, and especially not in the case of a complex domain.

Cialdini, who defined the seven influence levers we discussed in Chapter 14, describes a simple experiment to illustrate the power of contrast. Picture three buckets of water: hot, cold, and lukewarm. You put one hand in the hot water and another hand in the cold. You hold them in there for a minute and then put both hands in the lukewarm bucket. What you'll notice is a very different sensation in each hand. The actual temperature will be the same for both, but the perception will be wildly dissimilar. This is a powerful analogy for what happens in the informational world, too. We judge things on a contrast scale, not on an absolute scale, where the degree of change must be great enough for us to notice it.

This matters a lot to the sales professional, given all the competing demands on our clients' attention. As Dan Pink observed, "In the past, the best salespeople were adept at accessing information. Today, they must be skilled at curating it—sorting through the massive troves of data and presenting to others the most relevant and clarifying pieces."[1] In a world of information abundance, sales professionals create value by bringing more clarity rather than more content. Clients can't possibly sift through all the information themselves, and they rely on others to help them understand what is important.

Whether we're talking about the seller as Strategist, Change Agent, or Decision Architect, each of our three mental frames involves radical simplification to help the client. Strategists survey the external environment and identify the critical few levers that will strengthen the company's competitive position. Change Agents examine the organizational context and harness one or two pre-existing sources of energy. Within the interpersonal realm, Decision Architects pare down complexity into simple frames that get attention and drive action. Contrasting plays a major role in this process, and knowing how to contrast effectively is an essential selling skill.

One of the most famous examples of the contrast principle comes from an experiment that Dan Ariely ran with MIT students and summarized in his book *Predictably Irrational*.[2] Inspired by the effectiveness of an actual *Economist* subscription offer, he set out to establish whether he could maximize subscription revenue by presenting his students with the same options, working within the protocols of a controlled experiment. He divided a sample population of 100 students into two groups, and he showed three subscription options to Group A, then a separate set of options to Group B. The crucial difference between the two groups was that Group A got an extra "bundled" print and digital offer, whereas Group B simply had to choose between digital and print. You can see the percentage of students who chose each option in Table 16.1, below:

Table 16.1

GROUP A	GROUP B
Economist.com subscription – USD $59.00 16% *One-year subscription to Economist.com Includes online access to all articles from The Economist since 1997*	**Economist.com subscription – USD $59.00** 68% *One-year subscription to Economist.com Includes online access to all articles from The Economist since 1997*
Print subscription – USD $125.00 0% *One-year subscription to the print edition of The Economist*	**Print subscription – USD $125.00** 32% *One-year subscription to the print edition of The Economist*
Print & digital subscription – USD $125.00 84% *One-year subscription to the print edition of The Economist and online access to all articles from The Economist since 1997*	

The bundled offer made all the difference because it accentuated the contrast between the first and third options for Group A. They perceived the bundle as more valuable because it felt as though a digital subscription was being added "for free." Widening the contrast in this way boosted subscription revenue by 43 percent compared to Group B. Fundamentally, each group was being asked to choose between print and digital options, but the perception of those options was dramatically altered by a single variable.

One can apply these principles in a B2B context, where, again, it's important to simplify the confusion that often creeps into sales discussions. Clarity is what clients seek, and the mountain of information today is our common enemy. In many instances, the temptation in a B2B sales conversation is to present clients with a "comprehensive" view of their options. We want to be seen as thorough and complete. We want to defer to their judgment, ceding control of the decision variables. In almost all cases, however, this is a misguided approach.

Most of us have a sense of what it feels like when you are deeply motivated to buy, but a salesperson insists on complicating the purchase. I experienced this frustration while exploring options for the publication of this book. I decided I wanted to engage an independent publishing service, and I spoke with a sales representative from one of the top competitors in this space. I explained the book project, my goals, and what I was seeking from a publishing partner.

The person responded by sending the following table of pricing options. (See Table 16.2 on page 130.)

That was the moment I decided I wasn't going to be working with this company. Clearly, the sales representative hadn't listened to anything I had said. There was no attempt to curate the options based on my explicitly stated aims. It was a cookie-cutter reply, confirming that I wasn't working with a trusted advisor in any sense of the term. I saw this response as particularly poor form given my obvious intent to buy. I had made it *easy* for the seller. They had responded with a frame that was broad and complete, but utterly devoid of judgment as to what was important to me. It was the opposite of curation, and it cost that person a sale.

Typically, there are mental barriers that get in the way of a more simplified approach. For example, sellers might feel they are being manipulative if they exclude certain pieces of information. In theory, the suppression of data could be construed as deceitful. But in no way is it necessarily so. Further to Dan Pink's point, we need to distinguish between data suppression and data curation. It is the responsibility of sales professionals to exercise judgment, to use their discretionary authority. Their judgment should be a natural extension of the conclusions they have drawn from investigating the client's external and organizational dynamics. In principle, you should have a view on what makes sense for the company in your capacity as a Strategist and Change Agent. The options you present should reflect this view.

Table 16.2

	DISCOVERY	STARTER	ESSENTIAL
Original Price	**$999**	**$1,399**	**$2,199**
	30% OFF	30% OFF	50% OFF
Discounted Price	**$699.30**	**$979.30**	**$1,099.50**
1st Payment (Including $75 Fee)	$308.10	$401.43	$441.50
2nd Payment (Payable after 30 days)	$233.10	$326.43	$366.50
3rd Payment (Payable after 60 days)	$233.10	$326.43	$366.50
PUBLISHING FEATURES			
Digital Format & Distribution	√	√	√
Paperback Publishing	√	√	√
Hardcover Publishing	√	√	√
Cover/Interior Customization	√	√	√
Image Insertions	25	25	25
Electronic Proofs	√	√	√
Interior Revisions	√	√	√
Professional Marketing	√	√	√
One-on-One Support	√	√	√
Bookstore Availability	√	√	√

FUNDAMENTAL	CLASSIC VIP PACKAGE	PREMIERE VIP PACKAGE	OPTIMUM VIP PACKAGE
$3,199	$5,999	$8,899	$13,299
50% OFF	50% OFF	50% OFF	50% OFF
$1,599.50	$2,999.50	$4,449.50	$6,649.50
$608.17	$1,074.83	$1,558.17	$2,291.50
$533.17	$999.83	$1,483.17	$2,216.50
$533.17	$999.83	1,483.17	$2,216.50
PUBLISHING FEATURES			
√	√	√	√
√	√	√	√
√	√	√	√
√	√	√	√
50	50	75	100
√	√	√	√
√	√	√	√
√	√	√	√
√	√	√	√
√	√	√	√

I would have found it more compelling if the publishing salesperson had simplified my options in a way that aligned with my objectives. In general, I've learned and re-learned that a simple contrast of two to three possibilities is the best way to frame options for almost any client. Sure, there can be pushback. The person might ask why certain products or contract terms are not included in the pricing options. This gives you a chance to put on your Strategy and Change Agent hats. Strategically, you could make the case that "Option B" is best aligned with the client's scope of competition and what it will take for them to win. From a change perspective, the proposed term might reflect your understanding of what is most realistic, based on insights you've gathered from talking to key influencers in the organization. Being called upon to justify these curated options affords you the opportunity to showcase your business acumen. It sets you up to prove the extent to which you're dialed into the customer's external and organizational realities.

A final point about the Contrast Effect is that it shouldn't be reserved for pricing discussions at the end of a sale. Contrast is a form of framing, and framing is essentially the skill of selective emphasis. In this sense, sellers are engaged in framing from the moment of first contact with a customer. As we discussed in the previous chapter, selling can be seen as an extended series of conversations, and the ultimate direction of those conversations is significantly determined by the first few steps, much as lift-off calculations should be finely calibrated to prevent later distortions of a rocket's flight path. The Contrast Effect is an effective way to elicit an early judgment from customers.

Recall, for example, the discussion of Change Agent skills in Part II. We reviewed the story of how researchers used contrast to prime consumers before they eventually purchased milk at the grocery store. Over a period of weeks, a television campaign took the seemingly generic category of milk and drew a sharp distinction between a healthy and less healthy variety. To accentuate the distance between the two, they used lurid visuals that equated a glass of full-cream milk with five strips of bacon. In this case, and in many other retail cases, contrast was the primary mechanism to educate the buyer.

Similarly, in the early stages of an enterprise sale, the Contrast Effect can set the course of discussion with a client. One of the top performers I interviewed for this book discussed a scenario in which she inherited a commercial relationship that was apparently doomed from the start. This was a large enterprise customer who, in their introductory call, informed her matter-of-factly that they would be discontinuing their software subscription when the agreement expired in four months. They explained that her product was "essentially the same" as that of a competitor, and thus the leadership team had chosen the latter. With only a short stretch of time in which to regain the client's confidence, she immediately got to work. It was clear the client's perspective was based on a misunderstanding, and she used the Contrast Effect to educate them. She established criteria against which to judge the two products, based on what she knew was important to the company's growth agenda. She ran training sessions with various teams to make them aware of these points of comparison. By repeatedly emphasizing these differences in her training sessions, she created consensus on the comparative advantages of her company's solution. In short order, she had the usage data and field validation to back up her claims. With laser focus on the Contrast Effect, she quickly demonstrated the actual—and, for the client, previously unknown—differences between her product and the competition. Her win-back efforts led to a banner achievement, not only salvaging but also expanding the commercial relationship.

The Contrast Effect is a key part of a sales professional's skillset. It should be seen as an important ally in the quest to replace confusion with clarity. It should reflect your professional judgment, advancing the choices and trade-offs you perceive to be in your client's best interests, and consistent with the support they need to continue their change journey. But those who only use contrast in the closing stages of a sale are likely undermining their effectiveness. Many sales are lost ostensibly because of price objections, when in fact the client's decision is merely a way to rationalize a more fundamental misalignment that emerged earlier in the process. Contrast is a critical device for sharpening the client's judgment in a world that often overwhelms their ability to see clearly. Let's now look at a second principle that also helps you operate more effectively within the bounds of rationality.

CHAPTER 17

What's in a Name?

One of the recurring themes of this section is that as the information landscape becomes more crowded and complex, simplification becomes more necessary. One concept is better than three. A single sentence works better than two. A shorter word tends to land better than a longer one. As we work within the bounds of rationality, our challenge is to choose frames that facilitate fast judgment, but also serve the client's interest. This demands a careful and calculated choice of words.

We all recognize the power of words in politics and business. Political pollsters and market researchers assume, quite correctly, that the average person lacks the time and motivation to explore the nuances of any given topic. People look for an easy label to encapsulate everything they need to know about a given subject or personality. This explains why companies and political parties spend millions of dollars on focus groups each year, refining their terms to create specific impressions with the public.

One can feel a difference in the smallest tweaks to our language. Just pause for a moment and consider the different feelings that are evoked by these competing frames:

Used Car vs. Pre-Owned Vehicle
Death Tax vs. Estate Tax
Gambling vs. Gaming
Liberal vs. Progressive

It's completely irrational, but a "pre-owned vehicle" seems more attractive than a "used car." An "estate tax" feels like a reasonable price for the wealthy to pay, while a "death tax" feels arbitrary and unjust. "Gaming" comes across as more benign than "gambling." And who doesn't want to be considered "progressive"? In all cases, we are talking about *the same thing*, but our perception can be wildly different depending on the label that is used. The truth is that names capture and contain community norms.

People like Frank Luntz on the political right and George Lakoff on the political left have studied this fascinating phenomenon, and they have noted some important principles that contribute to mass perception. One of their general findings is that, on matters of public policy, outcome-focused labels work better than process-focused labels. So, for example, according to left-leaning voters in the US, the idea of "law enforcement" gets about 51 percent support in focus groups. But the notion of "halting violent crime" gets about 68 percent support, an increase of 17 percentage points. Meanwhile, among right-leaning voters, there is tepid support for the idea of "welfare" but significant support for "assistance to the poor."[1] The first term is an abstract concept that is open to individual interpretation, while the second term is a concrete outcome that is more likely to find universal appeal.

This has implications for business, too. Ask yourself how often you have used abstract terms like "digital transformation" or "operational efficiency." Could there be an outcome-focused label that shifts the client perception and creates broader endorsement? For example, do the goals of your initiative boil down to "finding more customers" or "closing deals faster"?

Outcome focus can apply at the product level, too. Frequently, when sellers reach out to prospects, they are making the case for change—in essence, a product or service to replace what is currently being used. As discussed in the previous section, "Becoming a Change Agent," proposing a change can trigger immediate, and often understandable, resistance. Changing the frame from product-led to outcome-led consideration can reduce the risk of such a response. For example, Harold Beck and Sons sells electric actuators for process control instruments. Their sales team routinely encounters aversion to change because the actuator is embedded in the specifications and procedures for other instruments. When Beck sellers approach a potential customer, they often hear statements such as "We already have actuators that are good enough." So they reframe their actuators' value by describing precisely what could go wrong and what it would cost the client: Motor failures would force unplanned maintenance, driving up production costs and reducing revenue.[2] This helps potential customers assess their needs more clearly, increasing their receptiveness to outreach from the Beck sales team.

Table 17.2 summarizes these important differences in framing.

Table 17.2

	ABSTRACT	CONCRETE
POLITICS	Law Enforcement (51% support) Welfare (23% support)	Halt Violent Crime (68% support) Help the Poor (68% support)
PROGRAMS	Digital Transformation Operational Efficiency	Find New Customers Close Deals Faster
PRODUCTS	Innovative Product Latest Technology	Component Failure Unplanned Costs

A key challenge for the Decision Architect is to come up with a simple reframe for your idea so that it takes hold within the bounds of rationality. There's a simple test to determine whether your efforts to "name and norm" have been successful. If you're successful, you will start to observe the client embracing your terminology. I can remember a scenario in which we saw this happening in a couple of ways. We had been discussing the possibility of a pilot program to test out our solution with a new client. Because we noticed strong pre-existing interest across their team, we decided to reframe this program as a "champion initiative" rather than a "pilot." In other words, we assumed—with good evidence—that our solution would be valuable to the client, and we positioned our early launch as a tactic to prepare for a broader rollout. The goal wasn't so much to test whether the solution worked, but to build a community of early advocates—"champions"—and to maximize momentum as we worked toward company-wide adoption. In addition to re-setting the frame in this way, we used a simple visual that showed how our solution mapped to the foundations of their existing technology stack. It was clear that our team had started to make significant traction with the client when we saw a copy of their internal pitch for executive approval. This pitch co-opted our "champion team" frame and repurposed the graphic that showed how we integrated with their technical infrastructure.

These were clear signs that our messaging had resonated. But that validation also showed another reason why simplicity is so important: For an enterprise sale especially, you are often relying on other people to make your case. If they are going to do an effective job at this, you need to make it as easy as possible for the client. The science is clear: Unaided recall of information received is abysmal, at less than 20 percent within a few hours, and only 2 to 3 percent within a month.[3] As Tim Pollard argues, the standard we should be shooting for is "retellability"—striving to make your story stick so well that it can be retold. It's largely *your* responsibility to create simple memes, labels, and visuals that travel easily within the organization. Keep it simple, avoid jargon, and engage your creative spirit to maximize your "naming and norming" impact. That is the mandate for a Decision Architect.

Bounds of attention are what define the context in which client judgements are made. As discussed, you can shape this context through well-selected points of comparison (Contrast Effect) or through labels that better frame the value of your product or service (Naming/Norming). The key point is that context is frequently susceptible to influence, and Decision Architects are on the lookout for opportunities to exert such influence. We turn now to the final two principles related to the bounds of self-interest.

CHAPTER 18

What Will They Lose?

What do the following three scenarios have in common? Exhibit A: Your friend has just encountered overwhelming evidence that disproves one of his long-held positions, but rather than concede the point he engages in elaborate intellectual contortionism to justify continued adherence to his original claim. Exhibit B: You bought a stock last year after getting a "hot tip" from some alleged authority, and although the price has since been falling precipitously you can't bring yourself to sell the shares. Exhibit C: You have a significant credit with a fancy resort because you were forced to cancel an all-inclusive vacation last year. The credit is about to expire, and you're now contemplating a different trip to a much more compelling destination, but you default to the original resort because you "already paid for it."

Each of these examples reveals a deeply entrenched cognitive bias known as loss aversion. Our aversion to loss is significantly more powerful than our desire for gain. Studies into loss aversion prove that the experience of earning an additional $100 is considerably less intense than the experience of losing $100 you already have.[1] Consciously and subconsciously, the dark cloud of loss eclipses the sunshine of gain.

This phenomenon plays out routinely in a company environment. In a 2012 study, McKinsey surveyed 1,500 managers, offering them a hypothetical chance to create $400 million of company value with a $100 million investment. The managers were asked what level of risk they would tolerate before approving such an investment. Rationally speaking, anything more than a 25 percent chance of success should be compelling, because 25 percent of the prospective $400 million is equal to the initial investment value. However, most of the managers indicated that they would only make this investment if it was at least 82 percent likely to succeed—three times higher than a risk-neutral position. When the investment was lowered to $10 million, with a potential $40 million gain, their response was the same.[2]

Daniel Kahneman once ran a similar experiment on a smaller scale, and he noted an interesting twist. He approached the direct reports of the CEO at a large corporation and presented them with a version of the above thought experiment. He offered each direct report a hypothetical opportunity to launch an initiative in their division that had a 75 percent chance of increasing profits and a 25 percent chance of causing a loss. Like the

McKinsey experiment, a substantial majority of these direct reports declined to launch the initiative, and specifically because they feared there was a one in four chance of getting fired.

But there was an interesting coda to those conversations. When Kahneman presented his findings to the full executive team, the CEO was taken aback. He declared that he would have wanted all his direct reports to approve the hypothetical initiative, because in the aggregate there was a higher probability that the company would be more profitable. The problem, of course, was that he could enjoy the fruits of aggregate gain without fearing the pain of individual loss. He had the luxury of a portfolio perspective while each of the VPs had seemingly been asked to make an independent decision. They felt they had to bear the brunt of the risk without the buffer of countervailing consequences across the team.[3]

Loss aversion is so powerful that it often creeps into processes that are ostensibly designed to mitigate its influence. It can pose a threat even when the buying committee is ostensibly committed to "objective" criteria. I recall the experience of a business development team that was pitching an innovative energy solution to a state utility. This team was competing against a traditional energy provider, and you would have been hard-pressed to design a more fact-based evaluation process. There were transparent criteria, external audits, and detailed discussions with the utility's technical team. After months of review, it was apparent that the new energy solution was scientifically and economically superior to the traditional alternative.

Behind the scenes, the utility's engineering organization gave their ringing endorsement. Yet, when the moment of truth arrived, the CEO announced his team had selected the traditional vendor.

It was a shocking revelation, one that defied any rational explanation. Eventually, the business development team understood their blind spot. They learned that the CEO was accountable to a board of directors whose perspective was skewed by industry veterans who were only comfortable with more established technologies. Given the strength of the board's influence, it was clear in hindsight that the process hadn't been designed to select the most compelling option. It had been designed to select the *least risky* option. Had the business development team understood this from the outset, they would have changed their approach. They would have focused on what the utility stood to *lose* by failing to select their technology, not just on what they stood to gain as a partner.

These stories reveal some crucial principles about corporate buying decisions. More often than we tend to assume, senior leaders approach decision-making through the lens of loss aversion. Rather than evaluate the likely success of an initiative, they are often more inclined to ask, "How will I be judged if I get this wrong?" And in many respects, that is a reasonable perspective, because the truth is that when a large-scale company initiative goes south it can tarnish the sponsor's reputation, if not lead to their dismissal.

This has practical ramifications for the way sellers frame their pitch in a B2B scenario. Rather than frame your product or service in terms of potential gain, it is often helpful to raise the consequences of inaction instead. For example, you might prompt a discussion about the potential loss to a decision-maker in three respects:

- *Competitors:* How could inaction give competitors a potential edge?

- *Colleagues:* How could inaction make other teams better equipped than yours?

- *Capabilities:* How could inaction remove specific product/service benefits?

I've seen two examples of this reframe with an enterprise software product that had a basic and advanced version. The typical way to promote the advanced version was to claim that the client would benefit from the additional capability of features x, y, and z. Then our team ran an experiment in which we shifted the focus from gain to loss. In differentiating the advanced from the basic version, we said that those who went with the basic product would lose the ability to use features x, y, and z. This led to a significant uptick in clients' interest in the advanced software.

Another example came on the heels of a trial phase in which we had run a large global pilot for the advanced version. When it came to the end of the pilot, we were working with the client's project team to prepare a renewal proposal. The project team was highly supportive of the renewal, but they were worried that their executive decision-makers would push back. To reduce the risks of rejection, they suggested reverting to the basic version of the software in our renewal proposal. We heard them out and agreed to pursue that path if it proved to be the only realistic option. But we first asked them to consider a draft that took a loss-based approach in defending the advanced version. This proposal enumerated several things that would be forfeited with a software downgrade. The project team was pleasantly surprised when their executive stakeholders offered no resistance to this argument.

There are three key takeaways here. First, many corporate decision-makers are inherently conservative because of loss aversion. (The once-common dictum—"No one was ever fired for buying IBM"—reflects the defensive nature of a corporate buyer's perspective.) Second, this conservative tendency is getting more pronounced because people must justify their decisions to a growing number of corporate stakeholders. (In a moment I'll address the growth trend in the average number of people involved in corporate decision-making.) Finally, loss aversion can be exacerbated or diminished depending on where the decision-maker falls in the hierarchy. In theory, loss aversion recedes as one climbs the corporate ranks, because an increase in authority implies an increase in scope, thus creating a stronger propensity for portfolio-based thinking. Compared to middle management, executives are more excited by possibility than risk. However, as the Kahneman example shows, the company culture plays a significant role, and many senior leaders live in constant fear of making the wrong decision.

Becoming a Decision Architect can't be dissociated from our overarching theme of plausible objectivity. The responsibility of the Decision Architect is to see the full field—both the seedbed of human nature and the climate that shapes the growth patterns you observe. The Decision Architect is ultimately responsible for driving action, and action is most reliably triggered when you can speak directly to someone's self-interest. That is partly a matter of understanding human universals, and it's partly a matter of being attuned to situational nuances. Let's look at a final principle that is all about connecting with someone's unique self-concept.

CHAPTER 19

How Do They See Themselves?

James Clear, the world-renowned expert on habit formation, has a perspective on identity with practical implications for the sales professional.[1] To understand the connection, first let's recall that one of the seller's most important responsibilities is to elicit information from helpful allies in the client organization. Because sellers are naturally disadvantaged as outsiders, they rely on internal advocates to help them navigate their customer's complex organizational reality. To be successful at this, sellers must learn to speak to the deepest sources of personal interest in a potential collaborator.

This is where Clear's insight is helpful. Let's assume you're attempting to engage a senior leader at a company. You believe this person can help you refine your sales thesis and possibly introduce you to other important stakeholders. Clear defines three levels of motivation as the basis for taking action: outcome, process, or identity. This framework also helps to understand why a senior leader might want to help you. Outcome reasons are the most superficial level of motivation. On this level you could be helping the person achieve specific company results, such as driving more revenue. Process is a slightly deeper level. On this level you could be helping the person reinforce company behaviors, such as a new way of engaging customers. Identity is the deepest level. On this level you could be speaking to the senior leader's self-image, helping them fulfill an aspirational commitment. This is the strongest level of motivation by far.

Clear's articulation of the power of identity is rooted in "role theory," a concept that first came to us from Erving Goffman, one of the most influential sociologists of the 20th century.[2] He theorized that we are all like actors on a stage, using "impression management" to present ourselves to others as we hope to be perceived. Role-related expectations are profound sources of influence because they embody layers of social consensus. They work on both a conscious and subconscious level, guiding us toward established patterns of behavior. As with many of the other psychological phenomena we've discussed, role-related instinct overpowers our conscious intent.

Working within the bounds of self-interest requires us to connect with the personal agenda of our clients. When it comes to fact-finding and discovery in sales, it's useful to have a simple frame that immediately speaks to a collaborator's personal interests. One of the most useful frames I've observed is that of the "expert"—making clients feel they are an authority, and then actively seeking their advice. This is a case of role theory in action, because to accept the role of an "expert" is implicitly to accept many deeply rooted assumptions.

Think for a moment about how you perceive experts, and how experts tend to view themselves. In the first place, an expert is someone who occupies an exclusive space. Experts represent a small minority of people who have acquired specialized knowledge or proficiency that is of value to the broader community. Second, experts have assumed obligations to that community. They are not expected to hoard their expertise like a hermit living high up on the mountainside. Experts derive meaning and fulfillment from sharing what they know with people who seek them out. Experts derive self-worth from a sense that they have been helpful to others. They feel successful when they make others successful. In many respects, the root psychology of experts is that they love to share what they've learned when they believe it will make a difference.

But there's another assumption that's built into the expert-apprentice dynamic. It's illustrated, as are so many other essential truths of human nature, in the *Star Wars* series. Yoda has just met Luke Skywalker in *The Empire Strikes Back*, and they have gotten off to an inauspicious start. Cooped up in Yoda's dim and diminutive dwellings, Luke is completely unaware that he's in the presence of someone who has trained Jedi masters for hundreds of years. Yoda encourages him to eat and rest, but Luke only becomes increasingly irritated. He starts to wonder why he's wasting his time with someone who looks nothing like the warrior he was expecting. He wants to cut to the chase, not waste time in idle conversation with this funny-sounding creature in the middle of nowhere. Despondently, Yoda looks off-camera, shakes his head, and says that he's not prepared to teach Luke. "The boy lacks patience," he believes.

Like most experts, Yoda will only agree to work with a newcomer when the newcomer has proven they are ready. Approaching client experts likewise demands a certain amount of preparation. It involves demonstrating you understand the expertise they have to offer, either based on publicly available information or personal testimony. It also involves earning their attention. Experts represent limited supply in a world of high demand. Their time is assumed to be at a premium, and they need to know that the person asking for help has warranted it. In general, when you approach any expert—client or otherwise—you should (a) show your work; (b) be respectful of the expert's time; (c) be precise in what you ask; and (d) follow up on the outcome.

Here's a framework that my team and I have used to approach client "experts." This structure is designed to improve your chance of securing a conversation, and to increase the value of your time with the expert. I credit Shane Parrish, creator of the excellent *Farnham Street* blog, for the initial inspiration behind this expert interview approach.[3] There are four components to this framework, and I'll summarize them below before discussing the key elements at play:

- *Goal:* "This is what we're working toward for mutual gain …"

- *Momentum:* "This is what we've accomplished so far …"

- *Frame:* "You're the expert in X. That's important because …"

- *Ask:* "If you were in our shoes, what would you do?"

GOAL: "This is what we're working toward for mutual gain ..."

Spelling out a clear goal up front is important for two reasons. First, it eliminates potential distractions during the conversation. You want the person to immediately understand the purpose of your discussion, avoiding the possibility that her mind will wander as she speculates about your underlying motives. Second, it shows respect. By getting to the point quickly, you implicitly indicate that you value the expert's time.

MOMENTUM: "This is what we've accomplished so far ..."

Explaining the momentum you've achieved so far—whether this means growing support for a new program or further traction within an existing program—accomplishes a couple of things as well. In general, people are more influenced by the direction of things than by the current status. Saying, *This initiative used to have a single sponsor, and now there are three divisions that have seen a 10x ROI* is more powerful than saying, *This program has a 10x ROI.* In a similar vein, saying, *Historically, we were only engaged with Jennifer in IT, but in the last six months Jane and Jim have been asking about how we can support their teams as well* is better than saying, *We're talking to Jennifer, Jane, and Jim.* Establishing momentum is also important to expert psychology because, as mentioned, experts want to make a difference. They can only advise a limited number of people, and they generally prefer to back people and initiatives that are more likely to have an impact. Momentum is a shorthand way to reassure them that this is a bet worth making.

FRAME: "You're the expert in x. That's important because ..."

Framing represents the crux of your interaction with the expert. This is where you precisely identify the expertise for which this person is widely respected, along with why it matters. Going back to the "influence levers" we discussed earlier in this section, calling out someone's expertise helps with likeability because the person is made to feel special. Crucially, however, this must be a legitimate claim, not just a sycophantic display of false admiration. There must be some basis for believing this person has unique insight, whether it relates to the latest technologies, the client's unique business processes, or specific organizational dynamics. The value of the "expert interview" is tightly correlated with the degree to which you've thoughtfully matched someone's unique value to the challenge you're facing. If an expert is well matched in this sense, then this conversation can save you hours—if not weeks—of effort.

ASK: "If you were in our shoes, what would you do?"

Since we are looking to maximize the value of our time with an expert, the way we ask for help is critically important. Asking "what" an expert would do is truly more of a "how" question. It engages the problem-solving part of the expert's brain, opening space for her to describe the decision variables and to explain which of them matter most. This allows you to probe her thought process, delving further into things that only a seasoned professional at this company could be expected to know. I've found that this open-ended question increases the expert's engagement and is most effective at revealing things that are difficult if not impossible to anticipate as a third party to the organization.

The role theory dimensions of the expert frame are ultimately a way to reverse the power dynamic in sales. Classically, when sales professionals engage senior influencers, the sales professional is at a positional disadvantage based on rank, tenure, and outsider status. Sellers often feel like supplicants at the dinner table, plaintively seeking leftovers from the king and queen. The expert frame turns this dynamic on its head, ceding power and prestige to the expert, but in a way that is most useful to the seller.

It bears repeating that this frame must be grounded in an honest assessment of the expert's unique strengths, how they map to your current impasse, and what the mutual benefits of collaboration are likely to be. A genuinely respectful relationship is the best use of the expert frame. This is also why follow-up matters a great deal. You will want to ensure the expert sees evidence that her help was effective, and you will want to continue to cultivate your relationship by affirming the value of her expert advice.

As the last of the six principles for the Decision Architect, this one completes our travels within the bounds of human cognition. We've discussed how to secure people's attention with Influence Levers and the Peak-End Rule. We've talked about how to focus their judgment with the Contrast Effect and Naming/Norming. We've covered how to speak more directly to their self-interest using the principles of Loss Aversion and Role Theory. These six principles are not exhaustive, as I said earlier. The three bounds encompass a much larger expanse than we've covered with the selection of only six principles. There is abundant space for further experimentation on the field. But seeing the field is the critical first step in cultivating a more objective mindset. Once again, let's bring some of these principles to life with the experience of a top performer. The following story stands out to me as a master class in the mindset and methods of a Decision Architect.

CHAPTER 20

The Decision Architect
in Action

Antonio is a senior sales professional who has a long history as an exemplary producer. He routinely exceeds the average quota attainment by anywhere from 20 to 300 percent. When questioned about his approach, he is decidedly other-centered: "I'm always there to be impressed, not to impress. I want to make the other person feel great." His company sells a multi-million-dollar technology solution within the financial services industry. There are dozens of features that one could conceivably cover in a demo, but Antonio quickly noticed that, from the customer's perspective, it is counterproductive to do so: "I could see that clients responded to a typical discovery call as if it were The Grand Inquisition. So, I started to pay closer attention to changes in their eyes and voice modulation. I started to look for their comfort zone. Where they want to focus is where I go."

One sale brings to life Antonio's unusually keen sensitivity to the interpersonal dynamics of a sale. He was working with a mid-sized American bank, and they had just hired a senior leader, Bruce, to manage one of the major US divisions. Whenever a new leader joins a client organization, it is always an important moment for the sales professional. New leaders are generally keen to make an impact, and they tend to look for early wins to set the tone of their company tenure.

But it's difficult to find time with a new senior leader who is frantically drinking from the firehose. Antonio needed to engineer an introduction and seed the idea of using his company's solution as part of an early-win agenda. He had a few relationships at the bank, and he knew that one of his contacts was expecting Bruce to attend a meeting on Friday. Antonio asked his contact if he could attend that meeting and give a brief overview of how his firm had been supporting the bank. He framed this as an opportunity to be part of Bruce's listening tour, giving him a more complete picture of the status quo across the bank's divisions. Antonio's contact agreed.

Antonio knew this would be a fleeting opportunity, and that he needed to carefully plan his messaging. He thought about his company's product and how it matched the strategic agenda of the bank. He knew that the speed of trade execution was a decisive factor in establishing a competitive advantage, and he understood this would be an important consideration for Bruce's division. But he was also conscious of the significant switching costs involved in selecting his company's solution. Assuming Bruce decided to make this switch, it would be closer to a heart transplant than a small incision. As Antonio thought about Bruce's perspective, he felt there would be an understandable resistance to the pain of "rip and replace."

Antonio determined that it would be unrealistic to expect anything close to an on-the-spot conversion of Bruce in their initial discussion. After all, he would only have a couple of minutes. Instead, he felt it would be better to tee up a subsequent conversation. So, he settled on two simple objectives. First, he wanted Bruce to feel in complete control. There would be no sales pitch, no pressure of any kind. Second, he would give Bruce a proverbial blank sheet with some dots on the page. In other words, instead of presenting a full "drawing" of how his solution mapped to Bruce's operational challenges, he would provide a few reference points and let Bruce make the connections for himself.

When it came time to engage with Bruce in the meeting, Antonio said something along the lines of "I know you're still in listening mode, and it will probably take more time to get all the details, but you may notice some inefficiencies." This was an example of dots on the page. Antonio didn't want to specify the precise nature of these inefficiencies, because he wasn't looking to make a hard sell. He just knew that Bruce was in the process of building a story about the status quo, and he suggested a way to think about one of the plot points in that story. He couldn't predict the details of Bruce's subsequent discoveries, but he knew that Bruce would be looking for problems to fix. He wanted to establish a connection between those problems and what Antonio might do to help.

However, as mentioned, there was also a psychological barrier associated with the expected switching costs of Antonio's solution. In priming Bruce, Antonio had to anticipate a likely resistance to change. He needed to proactively diminish that barrier, and he did so in the simplest of ways, by saying something like "The beauty of [his company's] implementation approach is that if everything isn't perfect, they take full responsibility for making it so." Antonio's statement was nuanced by design. First, he summoned the full power of his company in his characterization of their service promise. "They" and their brand were much bigger than him, enhancing the weight of this commitment. Second, he set the highest possible performance standard ("perfect"). Third, he explicitly removed the implementation burden from the client's shoulders.

Antonio accomplished his objectives in the introductory meeting. He gave Bruce a concise summary of the status quo, he primed him to identify opportunities for an early win, and he positioned himself as a potential partner with the institutional means to help. He waited just less than a week for Bruce to continue his listening tour, and he followed up with a short note asking whether Bruce would be interested in going deeper into potential ways of addressing some of the inefficiencies he might have found. By this point Bruce must have started to form his hypotheses, because he proposed a meeting on Friday afternoon that week.

The Friday meeting seemed to be a case of mixed signals. On the one hand, it was encouraging that Bruce had proposed a follow-up in such a short time. On the other hand, Friday afternoon was the worst possible slot on the work calendar. Things are typically relegated to late Friday because they have been displaced by higher priorities in the week. Friday afternoon is also a time when energy levels are low, with distracting thoughts about the weekend starting to intrude. The probability that this meeting would be cancelled at the last minute was despairingly high.

Friday morning came around. That's usually when executives scan their calendar for the day and make slash-and-burn decisions to free up time for unplanned events. Reassuringly, no request for a meeting cancelation came through. At around noon Antonio took a calculated risk, potentially losing the momentum he had gained this far. He sent Bruce a note saying, "I know we're on for this afternoon at 4:00, and that's still fine with me, but I want to make sure the meeting doesn't interfere with your plans for the weekend. If you'd prefer to get back to your family and re-schedule our discussion for next week, I completely understand." Bruce replied immediately, thanking Antonio for his consideration, and suggesting a lunch meeting the following Wednesday instead.

Antonio felt much better about the new arrangement, and he sensed that influence levers had played a role. It occurred to him that conceding time with Bruce's family was probably interpreted as a "gift" that called for reciprocation. The lunch offer felt like Bruce's attempt to even the interpersonal scales.

In preparing for the lunch meeting, Antonio once again relied on radical distillation. He made sure he was clear on the business needs and technical requirements that might come up, but he also thought about simple phrases that could travel with Bruce, who would have to represent these claims internally. He decided that the most memorable ideas had to be rooted in loss aversion, and he played with sound bites that captured key concerns he anticipated at the leadership level. For example, he thought about the risk of system breaks that aggravated customer relationships and ultimately cost money.

Antonio and Bruce met for lunch and had a rich discussion. A level of personal trust had already been established, and now Antonio deepened commercial trust by displaying genuine interest in Bruce's fresh perspective on the company. He asked about everything Bruce had learned so far. Then, offering his simple phrases, he provided a convenient clothing rack on which to hang these early impressions. At this point, Antonio's paraphrasing of the client's problems came across as valid encapsulations of what Bruce had observed, not as a presumptive diagnosis.

The lunch meeting confirmed the central features of a storyline for Bruce. Antonio had helped him see that a different system could drive different behaviors, which in turn could deliver better outcomes for the business. Bruce felt this story was worth presenting at the C-suite, and he invited Antonio to meet the executive team. Antonio said he would work with Bruce's assistant to set the meeting up, and that he would bring some of his colleagues to ensure all technical bases were covered. It was a clear validation that trust had been established.

When it came to the meeting, Antonio realized he was up against a fresh set of attention challenges. Six executive colleagues sat around the table, each of them preoccu-pied with their own agenda. He had to find a way to sync with these new stakeholders. After setting context for the meeting, Bruce gave Antonio the floor. Antonio proposed a round of introductions, asking everyone to explain their role, what they wanted to cover in the discussion, and any concerns they had coming into this meeting.

Antonio let people talk as much as they wanted. He knew that big titles have commensurately big egos that need space to move around. After each person had spoken, they waited for a response, but Antonio kept the introductions going in clockwise sequence around the table. He simply jotted down a word to summarize the key theme for each participant. After the last person had spoken, Antonio summarized their perspectives in serial fashion, previewing an answer that would be fleshed out by his colleagues in the room. There was a respectful silence around the table. It was clear the executives felt they had been heard. Antonio had earned the room's undivided attention.

After this tone-setting exercise, Antonio kept the focus on these stakeholder concerns, drawing from the team's expertise to satisfy the buying committee that day and beyond. In short order they had covered substantial ground. A typical sale at his firm takes about eight months, but in only a few weeks the bank had received a contract for sig-nature and the deal was done.

Antonio's experience underscores some important principles. He reminds us that customers don't just buy products; they also buy the person. And the shortest route to increasing trust and credibility as a person is to prioritize the perspective of others. It is the best way to maneuver within the bounds of attention, rationality, and self-interest. Antonio believes the executive committee moved so quickly because he inspired a feeling of confidence in them. It was this feeling he was after from the beginning, and it represents the target emotion of the Decision Architect.

Notice, too, how Antonio's story illustrates each of the mindset elements we've covered. As a Strategist, he first considered the client's external dynamics, coming quickly to terms with where they play and what it would take for them to win. As a Change Agent, he immediately identified where the energy for change was coming from, and he thought about how to feed that energy in his early interactions with Bruce. Finally, as a Decision Architect, he consistently asked what details mattered, and how he could get the client to care about those details. Significant preparation went into each major interaction as he thought about getting attention, simplifying choices, and harnessing self-interest.

The methods he used were context-specific, but they emerged from a distinctive mindset. I want to return to the idea of how mindset relies on first principles that are relevant to the evolution of sales and professional development more broadly. As we've discussed, first principles are the building blocks of knowledge. They are the most basic elements from which related concepts are derived. In the upcoming section, I conclude by linking the first principles of the Strategist, Change Agent, and Decision Architect to broader questions for the sales industry.

TAKEAWAYS FOR THE DECISION ARCHITECT

The Decision Architect's mindset prioritizes psychological principles to navigate three bounds of human cognition:

- *Bounds of Attention:* Economic and technological trends are progressively crowding out buyers' ability to stay focused. Brains are reductionist, fitting in is failing, and influence is transitory.
- *Bounds of Rationality:* After securing attention, remember that reason and emotion are deeply entwined. Truth is relative, facts don't matter, and reasoning is social.
- *Bounds of Self-Interest:* Converting attention to action is best achieved by tying your request to someone's self-interest. Everyone is the hero of their own feature film, heroes need constant reassurance, and self-preservation is primary.

Decision Architects ask, *What information is most important to the customer?* and *How can I get the customer to care about that information?* Use these six principles to navigate the bounds of human cognition:

Within the Bounds of Attention

- *Influence Levers:* How can I integrate social proof, authority, commitment and consistency, likeability, reciprocity, scarcity, and unity into my communications?
- *Peak-End Rule:* How can I maximize memorability and positive emotion in customer interactions?

Within the Bounds of Irrationality

- *Contrast Effect:* How can I widen the distance between proposed options?
- *Naming and Norming:* How can I use simple, outcome-focused labels that travel easily within the customer's organization?

Within the Bounds of Self-Interest

- *Loss Aversion:* How can I highlight the risk of potential losses over prospective gains?
- *Role Theory:* How can I use the "expert" frame to elicit insight and help from clients?

PART IV: WIDENING OUR LENS

"Today's problems can only be solved at a higher level of thinking than that which created them."

—ALBERT EINSTEIN

CHAPTER 21

The Tenets of Trust

The Sales MBA began by talking about a seller's progression from likeability to mutuality to objectivity. We observed that the highest level of sales performance is grounded in trust. Let's try to understand why. What is it about objectivity—and, specifically, a more objective view of the external, organizational, and interpersonal dynamics—that builds trust between the buyer and seller? If trust is the ideal end-state, it's worth breaking down the component parts.

To explore this theme, let's briefly consider one of most definitive references on the topic, *The Trusted Advisor* by David Maister, Charles Green, and Robert Galford. The book has been used for decades by consultants, lawyers, and other professional service providers. The authors' principal claim is that many professionals mistakenly assume mastery of technical content—simply "knowing your stuff"—is sufficient to earn the client's trust. The book counters this view by arguing that trust involves a separate set of skills, such as listening and engaging. The authors go on to say that even those skills are not enough. A trusted advisor must also have a particular mindset, one that includes self-confidence and curiosity, among other things. This is partly what inspired me to elaborate on the importance of mindset in this book.

Going back to first principles, let's ask ourselves a simple question: What is it that makes you trust another person in a professional context? To me, the clearest distillation—inspired by *The Trusted Advisor*—comes from Frances Frei and Anne Morriss in their *Harvard Business Review* article from 2020.[1] Frei and Morriss argue that people trust you when they believe you're giving them the real version of yourself (authenticity), when they respect your judgment and reasoning (capability), and when they sense you care about them (empathy). These three components are illustrated in Figure 21.1

Figure 21.1

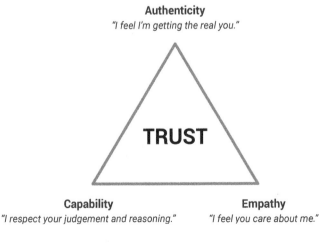

Authenticity
"I feel I'm getting the real you."

TRUST

Capability
"I respect your judgement and reasoning."

Empathy
"I feel you care about me."

If one of these elements is missing, then trust is unattainable. The three pillars are mutually reinforcing, and wobbliness in one area begins to undermine the overall effect. By the same token, earning trust requires a proportional emphasis on all three dimensions. They need to be manifested in a balanced and integrated way. You probably sense this is true, but let's flesh it out by playing with the dials on empathy, capability, and authenticity. In a sales context, what does it look like to have too much or too little of each?

Sellers who lack empathy tend to come across as self-serving. Generally, their lack of empathy stems from temperament or circumstances. Highly driven or overly analytical people, for example, can be oblivious to the client's deeper needs. But circumstances can also sabotage one's good intentions, given the frenetic nature of modern professional life. Even natural empaths can neglect the perspective of clients when time pressures push sellers to override their own instincts.

Can salespeople have too much empathy? Yes. Like each of the elements in the trust triad, you can overdo empathy if it comes at the expense of the others. It's not enough to care deeply about others. You must also show you can deliver. Perhaps you've had the experience of being sold to by someone who seemed to believe that a strong emotional connection was sufficient to justify a purchase, regardless of the strategic or financial rationale. It's not a good look. Sellers who over-index on empathy come across as naive.

As with empathy, a seller's lack of capability can be a deal-breaker. On the most basic level, sellers are expected to bring something of value to a business. Salespeople must be able to solve a problem, and ideally a significant one. This is fundamentally an issue of proving their capability. But exaggerated displays of capability can just as easily backfire, and I'll share a personal example to illustrate.

I had taken over the lead for my company's commercial relationship with a large supply-chain technology firm. My predecessor had built a strong relationship with the executive sponsor, but she hadn't yet developed a business case to demonstrate the substantial economic benefits of the program. My immediate impression was that this was an opportunity to showcase my analytical prowess, and to expand the commercial relationship to achieve an even greater ROI. I approached the business case with gusto, assembling a comprehensive package of qualitative and quantitative evidence to justify further investment in our services.

As I leaned back in my desk chair to ponder this analysis, I thought it was bulletproof. I proudly attached the deck to an introductory email to the executive sponsor, confidently requesting time to discuss how we could drive more value together. I honestly expected that he would be so taken by this proposal that he would plead for the first available slot on my calendar. Instead, he ignored me, and a couple of weeks later I learned through the grapevine that he deeply disliked the "pushy salesperson" he was now dealing with. Capability alone is a fool's errand.

A conspicuous lack of authenticity can also be disqualifying. In the first chapter I recounted the experience of being shut down by an executive because she correctly sensed that

I wasn't being straight with her. She was looking for an acknowledgment that I had a commercial agenda, and I insisted on sidestepping the question. Buyers, and especially executive buyers, are understandably repelled by sellers who shy away from the reality of personal incentives.

But this doesn't mean that buyers expect unadorned candor. As with the other two pillars, a singular focus on "telling it like it is" would be immediately damaging. No one is likely to warm to the sales professional who cuts to the chase by saying, *Now, let's be frank: My goal here is to get you to spend more money.* Your agenda must be balanced against the other two poles.

To summarize, when it comes to the conditions of trust, there can be too much or too little of a good thing. The triad calls for a careful coexistence of empathy, capability, and authenticity, as illustrated in Table 21.1:

Table 21.1 Balancing the Trust Triad

	TOO LITTLE	TOO MUCH	BALANCED
EMPATHY	Self-serving	Naïve	Caring but committed to proving value to the client
CAPABILITY	Unqualified	Pushy	Competent but committed to the client's deepest needs
AUTHENTICITY	Dishonest	Mercenary	Candid but committed to client outcomes as the measure of success

As we've observed, the career trajectory of top performers in sales has a consistent pattern. In the early stages of their career they focus on likeability, progressing to mutuality, and eventually achieving objectivity. In many respects this evolution is a matter of gradually erecting the pillars of trust. Early-career sellers tend to exaggerate the importance of interpersonal connection (empathy). Over time they get better at creating mutually beneficial outcomes, as they become more at ease with their personal agenda (authenticity). Ultimately, they refine the analytical and technical skills that create most value for their clients (capability). They become trusted advisors as they build and integrate the three components of the trust triad.

I'm revisiting the tenets of trust, and the delicate balance they require, to suggest that objectivity is what gets you to this point. It's only when sellers move from personal preoccupations to objective detachment that they can see how to balance and coordinate the disparate but interconnected components of trust. It's only then that they become trusted advisors. This is particularly important to remember as we think about the ongoing evolution of sales, which is what I'll discuss next.

CHAPTER 22

The Convergence of Consulting and Sales

I remember one of the first things that struck me when I made the transition from consulting to sales: Compared to the industry I had left behind, sales culture was manifestly more goal oriented. I was amazed by the apparently obsessive focus on "hitting one's number"—not just the quarterly or annual quota but also daily or weekly performance targets that determined who was on the leaderboard.

I became aware of how the underlying economic model had shaped this culture. In consulting, the key performance metric is utilization, or the percentage of a consultant's available time dedicated to billable work. That metric palpably plays out on the job. It explains why, from the time a consultant first meets her client, gripping his hand firmly and fixing him with a purposeful stare, she is acutely aware of being "on the clock." She senses a large, luminescent dollar sign above her head, and she's forever looking to justify her hourly rate. Moment by moment, her goal is to *keep adding value.*

In a sales context, I could see how a different economic model had created its own cultural norms. Quarterly revenue targets incentivize people to maximize outcomes within an arbitrarily short period. Salespeople are perpetually haunted by time limits, like someone who finds himself on a raft drifting downstream as the distant thunder of a waterfall grows louder and louder. The salesperson's goal is to *uncover value* as quickly as possible.

Both domains are high pressure, but in different ways. Consulting has traditionally attracted insecure overachievers. The stereotypical consultant seeks to dispel any doubts about their capability, and continually strives to exceed the client's expectations. Salespeople have generally been less interested in offering insight than eliciting it. Their priority has been to surface pain points and to deepen them through questioning. They too have been "on the clock," but with a more future-focused concern: getting to a signed contract.

Granted, there has long been a sales component in consulting. Partners and Senior Managers have always had to sell their next engagement. Similarly, much of the thought leadership in sales has emphasized the consultative dimension in challenging and educating one's customer. While this overlap has been evident for some time, consulting and sales have grown more alike in recent years because of informational and organizational trends that have brought their respective competency models closer together.

The information trend is very much related to the discussion about the "bounds of attention" in the previous section. Salespeople were once valued and recognized as custodians of specialized knowledge. Buyers needed sellers because sellers were deemed to have privileged access to restricted information. An obvious asymmetry of information access gave salespeople a degree of leverage with potential buyers. They were an important information node in the market for B2B products and services.

The Internet fundamentally changed this asymmetry. Sellers have been steadily losing leverage as information has become more widely and freely available. According to basic economics, the market value of something begins to decline when supply outpaces demand, and the profuse supply of online information has proportionally diminished many sellers' leverage. This helps to explain why, according to research from CSO Insights in 2017, attainment rates had declined for the five preceding years.[1]

These informational trends have also spawned organizational changes, which have further exacerbated the B2B sales challenge. In a world of growing information complexity, companies require new areas of specialized expertise to help them understand and compete in a rapidly evolving business landscape. Thus, the average number of executives reporting to the CEO has doubled in large companies from the 1980s through to the first decade of the 21st century.[2] These direct reports tend not to be generalists; they usually emerge from narrower domains, such as AI or data analytics.

Gartner, a global research and advisory firm, has been tracking the sales implications of these organizational changes for many years. In 2014, CEB (a Gartner subsidiary) reported an average of 5.4 people involved in corporate buying decisions.[3] According to their 2020 analysis, that number has increased to more than 11, and it approaches almost 20 in many B2B sales transactions.[4] Such developments make the job of a B2B sales professional substantially harder. The seller now contends with a more complex, interdependent, and nonlinear buying process, one in which a greater number of stakeholders have potentially conflicting perspectives on the core problem, solution requirements, and vendor selection criteria.

The initial response to these developments was to assume that B2B salespeople would inevitably become extinct. An article published by Forrester Research in 2015, "Death of a (B2B) Salesman," observed that in 2012 there were 4.5 million B2B salespeople in the US economy, according to the US Bureau of Labor Statistics. Forrester predicted that a million of those sales professionals— roughly a quarter—would lose their jobs to self-service e-commerce by 2020.[5] In fact, an analysis of 95 million online job postings in the United States from 2015–2018 showed double-digit *growth* for "sales reps" and "customer service representative" job titles.[6] Moreover, the skill categories in highest demand were "general sales practices" (9 percent annual growth), "general sales" (8 percent), and "basic customer service" (11 percent)—cumulatively the highest growth in desired skills across all job posting categories. In addition, whereas in 2016 only 54 percent of companies had a "Customer Success" function, by 2020 fully 96 percent of them did.[7]

At this point we should have a more nuanced appreciation of what has been happening. It seems fair to say that B2B selling is getting much, much harder—but no less important. Selling is harder because information is more abundant and company decision-making is more complex. But selling is equally important *for the very same reasons.* Information abundance and the speed of technology evolution have intensified competition. B2B sales organizations have therefore been forced to think more like consultants. Increasingly, their overarching goal is to *keep adding value* because, under today's market conditions, if you cease to be valuable to your customers, they will simply repurpose their budgets. There are too many innovations happening all around to privilege an incumbent vendor over the growing array of compelling alternatives.

This seems to explain why so many companies and sales organizations are now laser-focused on The Customer. An emphasis on "outcome-focused selling" and "customer success" is a key part of the growing recognition that post-sales activities matter as much as—if not more than—what led to a signed contract. Pre- and post-sale, B2B sellers are subject to more intense scrutiny as they seek to satisfy multiple stakeholders. To be credible with a wider range of buyers and influencers, sellers require higher levels of sophistication in their understanding of external, organizational, and interpersonal dynamics. It makes sense, therefore, that we would see a decline in transactional selling roles, which are indeed better matched with self-serve e-commerce models. But it also makes sense that these staff reductions would be offset by a roaring demand for more consultative selling skills.

That is why I believe we need to revisit the first principles of sales. As selling becomes a more high-stakes function, and as sales skills are an increasingly important part of the knowledge worker's talent stack, I believe we need a new teaching model. There is much to be learned from an adjacent area like consulting, given its central preoccupation with adding value. The sales industry needs a fresh set of organizing principles that apply to B2B sales. These principles must be specific enough to capture common themes, but broad enough to allow for context-specific adjustments. As an industry, sales must start to build consensus around such principles, so that we can scale a curriculum that better serves the knowledge worker community—those who carry a quota and those who sell and influence as part of their job.

Again, I believe the consulting space provides some useful points of reference. The new competency model for an enterprise seller should be reminiscent of what we tend to see in the consulting space. Sellers need to be externally adaptable across a range of industries, verticals, companies, business units, and clients. They should also be internally versatile, capable of maximizing the value of company assets by proactively seeking help from colleagues to better serve the customer. As the trust triad shows, the effectiveness of trusted advisors extends far beyond their ability to prove they know their stuff. Trust is grounded in a certain mindset, from which specific thinking and behavior tend to follow.

The Sales MBA's organizing principles—Strategist, Change Agent, Decision Architect—are what I propose as the first step on the road to a new pedagogy for B2B sales. It is influenced by what I've seen and experienced as a consultant, but it's also tied to bigger and broader claims. I'll close by explaining what I think those are.

CHAPTER 23

The Laws of Life

I've long been fascinated by "fractals"—the idea that deep truths are revealed at varying levels of analysis. The micro mirrors the macro, and vice versa. In physics, for example, electrons orbit the nucleus of an atom just as planets orbit the sun. In literature, a single passage can reveal how to read the rest of the novel more insightfully. In biology, the tiniest sample from a living body—flesh, bone, saliva—reveals the DNA of the whole organism. A fractal is a rule that is iteratively applied across the pattern of reality, making that pattern endlessly varied but also endlessly similar.

Captain B. H. Liddell Hart, the famous British historian and military theorist, once described the excitement of discovering a fractal truth as he got closer to the essence of military strategy:

> When, in the course of studying a long series of military campaigns, I first came to perceive the superiority of the indirect over the direct approach, I was looking merely for light upon strategy. With deepening reflection, however, I began to realize that the indirect approach had a much wider application—that it was a law of life in all spheres: a truth of philosophy.[1]

I can relate to this feeling. Stumbling upon a fractal truth triggers a sense of wonder and awe at the profound connectedness of the world. I've had this experience while thinking about the three core elements of *The Sales MBA*. I've noticed that what makes a successful enterprise sales professional is reflected across adjacent realms in life and work. Observing the interconnections has given me a greater appreciation for the power and potential of the principles we've discussed.

To show you what I mean, let's temporarily depart from the world of B2B sales and reflect on the impressive career trajectory of comedian, actor, writer, and producer Jerry Seinfeld. You'll notice that Seinfeld intuitively applied the concepts of this book, becoming a Strategist, Change Agent, and Decision Architect to achieve astonishing levels of success.

SEINFELD AS STRATEGIST

Remember that Strategists ask *Where do I compete?* and *How do I win?* Seinfeld had the benefit of an epiphany early in his life. He came across a book on the craft of stand-up comedy (*The Last Laugh*, written by Phil Berger) and a movie about the industry (*Lenny*, directed by Bob Fosse). These serendipitous discoveries triggered a realization: "Oh my god," he thought to himself. "I want to do that."[2] It became clear to him that comedy was the space in which he would plant his flag as a competitor.

Having thus defined his area of competition, Seinfeld set out to determine what it would take to win. He watched the greatest stand-up comedians at the time and saw that many things came together in a successful performance: writing, delivery, physicality, audience connection, among other things. Making the crowd laugh was a matter of balancing these variables in real time. It was a context-specific craft. But Seinfeld determined that writing was the lead variable in this equation. He committed to systematically improving his ability as a writer, sensing that this would give him the strongest competitive advantage on a noisy playing field.

SEINFELD AS CHANGE AGENT

Remember that Change Agents ask, *Where is the energy for change coming from?* and *How can I feed that energy?* Seinfeld realized that, if he had any hope of changing himself as a writer, he needed a methodical approach that would rewire his brain. Intentions alone would not suffice. So, he built a program for behavioral modification, incorporating all six of the dimensions discussed in Part II. This program, revealed in interviews that coincided with the release of his autobiography, helped him progress from self-doubt to self-confidence as a comedy writer.

Maximizing engagement

Seinfeld identified a deep emotional need, which was to explore the hidden meaning of seemingly unremarkable events. Scenes and moments in *The Last Laugh* and *Lenny* tripped something in his head, and he couldn't help but pursue what had gripped his attention. In his autobiography, *Is This Anything?*, he describes the "absolute lack of glamour" and the "normalcy" that "drove me wild," hinting at the prosaic themes that came to characterize his stand-up and television material. He had found a reason to pay close attention to these everyday phenomena.

Minimizing complexity

Seinfeld simplified his process. Moving from amateur to professional required a step change in his writing ability. It involved working toward an end-state so far beyond his current capability that the distance could have been dispiriting. He committed to a simple protocol that involved a fixed time to write each day. There was just one governing rule: He couldn't do anything but write in that time. He didn't *have* to write, but he couldn't do anything else. The simplicity of that routine organized his mind, establishing a repeatable mechanism to build compound returns.

Enlisting influencers

Seinfeld used social factors to drive and sustain his success. He moved to LA and became part of the lineup at The Comedy Store, considered the marquee feeder school for professional comics at the time. He was soon surrounded by other people whose talent and ambition he hoped to absorb. Things went sideways after a clash with the owner, and Seinfeld walked away from The Comedy Store in protest to its management philosophy. That decision could have been career suicide, but the confrontation created its own kind of "negative" social influence, powerfully motivating him to prove to his former boss that she had messed with the wrong person. The intensity of this new-found, and highly personal, motivation had the effect of doubling his creative output.

Enabling collaboration

Seinfeld created a feedback system to accelerate his improvements. Using the audience as collaborators, he meticulously refined his material in rinse-and-repeat fashion. He would test out bits on stage, carefully note the reactions in the room, then return to the desk to rework his material, abandoning the dead-enders and polishing the few diamonds in the debris. As avowedly self-reliant as the confrontation with The Comedy Story owner had made him, collaboration with the audience became an indispensable contribution to his ultimate mastery as a writer.

Incentivizing behavior

Seinfeld built a reward system to sustain his motivation. After completing his daily writing quota, he put a red X in the day box of a calendar he kept prominently displayed in his apartment. Over time, as the uninterrupted chain of X's grew, visual evidence of his consistency became a compounding source of inspiration. He took what needed to be done and turned it into a game. He used simple, structural rewards to create dopamine effects that nourished a new habit.

Shaping context

Seinfeld manipulated his environment to reinforce the right behavior. It wasn't just that he had a simple write-or-do-nothing rule for his daily routine. He was also very deliberate about shaping a physical context that would nudge him in the direction of greater productivity. He carefully arranged the key variables to conserve mental energy: chair, desk angle, coffee mug selection, paper pad placement, and so forth. Exploiting these features of his environment limited his attention but deepened his focus on the most important things.

With this systematic approach to self-improvement, Seinfeld continuously nourished his own energy source. He took a deep emotional need and gave it a vehicle for expression. He took pre-existing motivations and built social support mechanisms to pursue them. He dug trenches on either side of the road to success, ensuring he stayed on the straight and narrow. Beyond these personal, social, and structural pillars, he was extremely adept at managing his own psychology.

SEINFELD AS DECISION ARCHITECT

Remember that Decision Architects ask *What details are worth emphasizing?* and *How can I get others to care about those details?* Seinfeld's story is teeming with examples of reframing. Granted, his stage and TV material is all about transforming the ordinary into the hilarious. But behind the scenes, too, he was masterful at selective emphasis to redirect and refocus his energy. He adroitly managed his own psychology, and this was a key part of what built and sustained his creative momentum.

Most notably, Seinfeld made frequent use of The Contrast Effect throughout his career, deliberately constraining his perspective to avoid the immobilizing effects of cognitive overload. He expressly preferred the simplicity of either/or options, saying, "I don't want too much mental freedom. I have too much of that anyway."[3] He routinely generated A-or-B constructs to shape his attitude and compel his decisions. Faced with the potential stress of having to prove himself to a room full of strangers each night, he framed the alternative as worse: "I was more than happy to accept being a not-that-funny comedian over any other conceivable option."[4]

He describes his writing process as a Jekyll-and-Hyde struggle, flipping back and forth between nurturing himself in the creative phase—when his ego needs to be treated like a toddler—and harshly criticizing himself in the editing phase, when he feels it's better to be pushed around by a "hard-ass." In advising others, he also defaults to contrast principles as the most effective way to support their creative journey. Attempting to motivate his teenage daughter, for example, he explains that having a creative talent is like owning a powerful black stallion: You either learn to ride the animal or it kills you.[5]

Contrasting imposes simplicity on the complex, highlighting one or two features in a seemingly reductionist manner. That is the essence of Seinfeld's skill as a stand-up artist, but also as a world-class performer in his domain. He plays with the perceptual frame to see reality more clearly and constructively, pushing himself to perpetually improve.

There's an irony about invoking Seinfeld toward the end of a book on how to sell more effectively to corporate clients. Seinfeld was once interviewed by *Harvard Business Review*, and he was asked whether a top strategy consulting firm might have helped him avoid the burnout that ultimately brought his legendary television series to a close, much to the disappointment of adoring fans.[6]

> **HBR:** Was there a more sustainable way to do it? Could McKinsey or someone have helped you find a better model?
>
> **Seinfeld:** Who's McKinsey?
>
> **HBR**: It's a consulting firm.
>
> **Seinfeld:** Are they funny?
>
> **HBR:** No.
>
> **Seinfeld:** I don't need them. If you're efficient, you're doing it the wrong way. The right way is the hard way. The show was successful because I micromanaged it: every word, every line, every take, every edit, every casting. That's my way of life.

Seinfeld had no time for experts on corporate efficiency, so how could corporate professionals have anything to learn from him? What does the fractal similarity between Seinfeld's approach and the three core frames of this book reveal? In addition to deeper concept validation, I think it highlights an inescapable tension between creative and procedural work. Seinfeld recoiled at the idea that his creative output could be standardized with the help of strategy consultants. His approach was too customized and crafts-man-like to be amenable to their advice. But of course, as we've just observed, Seinfeld was in fact highly systematic and procedural. It is hard to imagine anyone with a stronger craving for systems and structure.

In the world of B2B selling, there is likewise a tension between process and creativity. There are many books and resources that prescribe a stepwise formula for driving and consummating a corporate deal. *The Sales MBA* is not one of them, and that isn't because there is anything intrinsically wrong with those approaches. Playbooks encapsulate settled wisdom and proven results. No one should work entirely from first principles, since we need to build on what others have already figured out. But nor should anyone rely exclusively on predefined formulas, since conventional wisdom can only be partially correct. It's important to regularly revisit the bigger picture. That is the essence of what *The Sales MBA* sets out to do. This book is about returning to the source material for innovation in sales. The goal has been to expand your awareness of the external, organizational, and interpersonal factors at play, and to push the confines of your creativity.

That brings us full circle to the cook versus chef comparison from the introduction to this book. In any complex domain, there will always be playbooks and recipes to navigate the messy reality. Enterprise selling is certainly such a domain, since closing a B2B sale involves a non-linear sequence of conversations in a dynamic environment. Some of that sequence can be managed in advance, and some of it is beyond what such processes can ever anticipate. The enterprise seller constantly chooses between copying and creating. My hope is to help you see the field clearly and from scratch, so that you better understand—or perhaps rediscover—the first principles of sales success.

THE SALES MBA READING LIST

BECOMING A STRATEGIST

Core Readings

Aligning Strategy and Sales by Frank Cespedes

Playing to Win by Roger Martin

Good Strategy Bad Strategy by Richard Rumelt

Supplementary Readings

Steve Jobs by Walter Isaacson

The Everything Store by Brad Stone

The Practice of Management by Peter Drucker

Measure What Matters by John Doerr

The Strategy Paradox by Michael Raynor

The Strategy of the Indirect Approach by Liddell Hart

Crossing the Chasm by Geoffrey Moore

BECOMING A CHANGE AGENT

Core Readings

Switch: How To Change Things When Change is Hard by Chip and Dan Heath

Influencer: The New Science of Leading Change by Joseph Grenny, Kerry Patterson et al.

Supplementary Readings

Leading Change by John P. Kottler

The Heart of Change by John P. Kottler

Flat Army: Creating a Connected and Engaged Organization by Dan Pontefact

Reinventing Organizations by Frédéric Laloux

The Power of Positive Deviance by Richard Pascale, Jerry Sternin et al.

Getting Change Right by Seth Kahan

BECOMING A DECISION ARCHITECT

Core Readings

Influence: The Psychology of Persuasion by Robert Cialdini

Thinking Fast and Slow by Daniel Kahneman

Predictably Irrational by Daniel Ariely

Nudge by Richard Thaler

Supplementary Readings

How We Decide by Jonah Lehrer

Contagious: Why Things Catch On by Jonah Berger

Sway: The Irresistible Pull of Irrational Behavior by Ori Brafman

The Enigma of Reason by Hugo Mercier

The Person and The Situation by Lee Ross

Metaphors We Live By by George Lakoff

Words That Work by Frank Lutz

Strangers to Ourselves: Discovering the Adaptive Unconscious by Timothy Wilson

Alchemy by Rory Sutherland

Pre-suasion by Robert Cialdini

WIDENING OUR LENS

The Trusted Advisor by David Maister

ACKNOWLEDGMENTS

Book-writing is a deceptively solitary endeavor. It's tempting for observers to assume the author made it to the mountaintop through sheer grit and force of will. The truth is that many people have been cheering me on at the base, and several supporters have manned the rest stations along the way. I'm profoundly grateful to all of them.

Most importantly, I want to thank Alyssa Merwin and Brian Walton at LinkedIn for supporting a book-writing sabbatical. When I asked them about taking a quarter off to complete this manuscript, they immediately endorsed the idea. (Although, as happy as I was with that decision, I couldn't help but recall the late Canadian professor Hugh Kenner, who once reported that whenever he approached the university administration to request a leave of absence, he found them insultingly cooperative!)

I want to thank Ann Maynard at Command +Z Content for providing such excellent editorial advice. I'm grateful to have found someone so intensely committed to craftsmanship, and who instantly got what this book was about. She pushed and inspired me to expand my creative self to a degree that has fundamentally redefined my sense of what the future may bring. Ann makes you feel uncomfortable in the best possible sense.

Frank Cespedes at Harvard Business School first inspired the intellectual journey that led to *The Sales MBA*, and he was generous enough to review an early draft of the manuscript. Frank's course and writings have greatly influenced my perception of the linkage between strategy and sales. In addition, he has set a new standard for teaching. If I can approximate a portion of his classroom impact, I will consider that a career-defining achievement.

John Beshears, Co-Chair of the HBS Behavioral Economics department, was tremendously helpful and supportive as an early reviewer as well. His course and feedback were particularly important to the Decision Architect section. And I benefited from of all the great questions and comments from John's students.

Several current and former LinkedIn colleagues provided highly constructive feedback: Richard Wiltshire, Jeff Becker, Alison Schutz, Shaun Burns, John Mayhall, Eric Becker, Sam Lewis, Alex Moya, Audrey Lowder, Kalsang Tanzin, and Evan Kelsey were especially insightful.

I've long believed that teaching helps the teacher as much as the student, and I've learned so much from my students at Ryerson's DMZ program and the Rotman

School of Management, University of Toronto. They helped to iterate this content with their first-rate questions and critiques.

Finally, I want to thank my wife, Katherine, and my daughters, Iliana and Alexandra, for their patience. A project of this magnitude demands extreme focus, which can't help but strain family dynamics at times. These women have accommodated a challenging schedule and sustained my motivation with their quiet confidence throughout. They are the sun of my solar system.

NOTES

The Mindset Advantage

1   Daniel H. Pink, *To Sell Is Human: The Surprising Truth About Moving Others* (New York: Riverhead Books, 2012), chap. 1, Kindle.

2   Frank V. Cespedes, *Sales Management That Works: How To Sell In A World That Never Stops Changing* (Boston: Harvard Business Review Press, 2021), chap. 2, Kindle.

3   Oliver Burkeman, *Four Thousand Weeks* (New York: Farrar Straus and Giroux, 2021), Kindle.

4   Tim Urban, "The Cook and the Chef: Musk's Secret Sauce," *Wait But Why* (blog), December 15, 2019, https://waitbutwhy.com/2015/11/the-cook-and-the-chef-musks-secret-sauce.html.

Chapter 1

1   "Vision Statement," Ikea, accessed March 1, 2022, https://www.ikea.com/gb/en/this-is-ikea/about-us/the-ikea-vision-and-values-pub9aa779d0#:~:-text=%E2%80%9CTo%20create%20a%20better%20everyday,more%20sustainable%20life%20at%20home.

2   "Mission Statement," Patagonia, accessed March 1, 2022, https://www.patagonia.com.au/pages/our-mission.

3   Lawrence Freedman, *Strategy: A History* (Oxford: Oxford University Press, 2013), chap. 20, Kindle.

4   Walter Isaacson, *Steve Jobs* (New York: Simon & Schuster, 2011), chap. 26, location 5735, Kindle.

5   Chris Anderson's *The Long Tail* discusses this point at greater length, and it remains a must-read for making sense of the Internet-based economy.

6   Brad Stone, *The Everything Store: Jeff Bezos and the Age of Amazon* (New York: Little, Brown and Company, 2013), Prologue, location 143, Kindle.

Chapter 2

1   Peter F. Drucker, *The Essential Drucker: The Best of Sixty Years of Peter Drucker's Essential Writings on Management* (New York: Harper, 2014), Kindle.

2   See interview with Airbnb's co-founder Brian Chesky on Reid Hoffman's *Masters of Scale* podcast: https://mastersofscale.com/brian-chesky-handcrafted/.

3   Robert Simons, "Stress-Test Your Strategy: The 7 Questions to Ask," *Harvard Business Review*, October 24, 2020, https://hbr.org/2010/11/stress-test-your-strategy-the-7-questions-to-ask.

Notes 203

Chapter 3

1 Geoffrey A. Moore, *Crossing the Chasm: Marketing and Selling Disruptive Products to Mainstream Customers.* Third Edition. (New York: HarperBusiness, 2014), Introduction, Kindle.

2 Geoffrey A. Moore, *Crossing the Chasm: Marketing and Selling Disruptive Products to Mainstream Customers* (New York: HarperBusiness, 2014), chap. 6, location 2442, Kindle.

3 Moore, *Crossing the Chasm*, chap. 6, location 2335, Kindle.

Chapter 5

1 Roger Banister was a British Olympic runner who ran the first sub–4-minute mile in 1954.

Chapter 6

1 *Breaking Bad*, season 1, episode 1, "Pilot," created by Vince Gilligan, aired January 20, 2008, on AMC (High Bridge Productions, 2008).

2 Jonah Berger, *The Catalyst: How to Change Anyone's Mind* (New York: Simon & Schuster, 2020), Introduction, Kindle.

3 *The Simpsons,* season 22, episode 3, "MoneyBart," created by Mark Kirkland, featuring Dan Castellaneta, Julie Kavner, Nancy Cartwright, Yeardley Smith, and Harry Shearer, aired October 10, 2010, on Fox Broadcasting Company.

Chapter 7

1 Kevin Kelly, *The Inevitable: Understanding The 12 Technological Forces That Will Shape Our Future* (New York: Penguin Random House: 2016), chap. 3, location 933, Kindle.

Chapter 9

1 Go to YouTube and search "Candid Camera social conformity."

2 Joseph Grenny, Kerry Patterson, David Maxfield, Ron McMillan, and Al Switzler, *Influencer: The New Science of Leading Change*, 2nd ed. (New York: McGraw-Hill Education, 2013), chap. 6, Kindle.

3 See, for example, Richard Koch and Greg Lockwood, *Superconnect: Harnessing the Power of Networks and the Strength of Weak Links* (Toronto: McClelland & Stewart, 2010), chap. 2, location 432, Kindle.

4 Patterson et al., chap. 6.

5 Patterson et al., chap. 5.

6 The 80/20 principle states that surprisingly few inputs (20 percent) tend to generate most of the outputs (80 percent). To dig deeper, see Richard Koch, *The 80/20 Principle: The Secret to Achieving More with Less* (New York: Crown Publishing Group, 2017), Kindle.

Chapter 10

1 Timothy D. Wilson, *Strangers to Ourselves: Discovering the Adaptive Unconscious* (Boston: Harvard University Press, 2004), chap. 5, Kindle.

Chapter 11

1 Joseph Grenny, David Maxfield, and Andrew Shimberg, "How to Have Influence," *MIT Sloan Management Review* 50, no. 1 (Fall 2008).

2 Janice Thomas, Connie L. Delisle, Kam Jugdev, and Pamela Buckle, "Selling Project Management to

Senior Executives" (paper presented at PMI® Research
Conference 2000: Project Management Research at the
Turn of the Millennium, Paris, France. Newtown Square,
PA, June 24, 2000), https://www.pmi.org/learning/library/
selling-project-management-senior-executives-143

Chapter 13

1   See Richard H. Thaler, *Misbehaving: The Making of
Behavioral Economics* (New York: W.W. Norton: 2015),
chap. 27, location 4070, Kindle.

2   Tim Pollard, *The Compelling Communicator: Mastering
the Art and Science of Exceptional Presentation Design*
(Washington, DC: Condor House Press, 2016), chap. 9,
location 1985, Kindle.

3   Daniel Kahneman, Olivier Sibony, and Cass R. Sunstein,
Noise: A Flaw in Human Judgment (New York: Little,
Brown & Company, 2021), chap. 24, Kindle.

4   For an elaboration of this theory, see Hugo Mercier, *The
Enigma of Reason* (Boston: Harvard University Press, 2017),
Kindle.

5   Kahneman, Sibony, and Sunstein, chap. 20.

Chapter 14

1   Daniel Kahneman, *Thinking, Fast and Slow* (New York:
Farrar, Straus and Giroux, 2011), pt. I, Kindle.

2   David B. Strohmetz, Bruce Rind, Reed Fisher, and
Michael Lynn, "Sweetening the Till: The Use of Candy
to Increase Restaurant Tipping," *Journal of Applied Social
Psychology* 32 (2002): 300–309, https://files.secure.website/
wscfus/5261551/uploads/Candy_Manuscript.pdf.

Chapter 15

1 D. A. Redelmeier, J. Katz, and D. Kahneman, "Memories of Colonoscopy: A Randomized Trial," *Pain* 104, nos. 1–2 (July 2003): 187–94, doi: 10.1016/s0304-3959(03)00003-4.

Chapter 16

1 Daniel H. Pink, *To Sell Is Human: The Surprising Truth About Moving Others* (New York: Riverhead Books, 2012), chap. 6, Kindle.

2 Daniel Ariely, *Predictably Irrational: The Hidden Forces That Shape Our Decisions* (New York: HarperCollins, 2010), chap. 1, Kindle.

Chapter 17

1 Frank Luntz, *Words That Work: It's Not What You Say, It's What People Hear* (New York: Hyperion Books, 2010), chap. 2, location 1073, Kindle.

2 Frank Cespedes and David Hoffeld, "Reframing Value in a Crisis," *Top Sales Magazine*, July 2020.

3 Tim Pollard, *The Compelling Communicator: Mastering the Art and Science of Exceptional Presentation Design* (Washington, DC: Condor House Press, 2016), chap. 6, Kindle.

Chapter 18

1 Daniel Kahneman, Jack L. Knetsch, and Richard H. Thaler, "Anomalies: The Endowment Effect, Loss Aversion, and Status Quo Bias," *The Journal of Economic Perspectives* 5, no. 1 (Winter 1991): 193–206.

2 Dan Lovallo, Tim Koller, Robert Uhlaner, and Daniel Kahneman, "Your Company Is Too Risk Averse," *Harvard Business Review*, March–April 2020. https://hbr.org/2020/03/your-company-is-too-risk-averse.

3   Rory Sutherland, "The Objectivity Trap: On the Biases and Misconceptions That Cause Us All to Undervalue B2B Marketing," *The B2B Institute of LinkedIn*, last modified July 2020, https://www.ogilvy.com/ideas/objectivity-trap.

Chapter 19

1   James Clear, "Identity-Based Habits: How to Actually Stick to Your Goals This Year," accessed February 15, 2022, https://jamesclear.com/identity-based-habits.

2   Erving Goffman, *The Presentation of the Self in Everyday Life*, (New York: Random House, 1959), Kindle.

3   FS Courses, "Decision by Design," accessed February 15, 2022, https://fscourses.com/p/decision-by-design-sign-up-now.

Chapter 21

1   Frances X. Frei and Anne Morriss, "Begin with Trust," *Harvard Business Review*, May–June 2020.

Chapter 22

1   "Running up the Down Escalator, 2017 CSO Insights World-Class Sales Practices Report," CSO Insights, accessed March 5, 2022, https://pleinairestrategies.com/wp-content/uploads/2017/12/2017-World-Class-Sales-Practices-Summary-Report.pdf.

2   Cespedes, chap. 11.

3   Nicholas Toman, Brent Adamson, and Cristina Gomez, "The New Sales Imperative," *Harvard Business Review*, March–April 2017, https://hbr.org/2017/03/the-new-sales-imperative.

4   "5 Ways the Future of B2B Buying Will Rewrite the Rules of Effective Selling," Gartner, August 4, 2020, https://www.gartner.com/en/documents/3988440/5-ways-the-future-of-b2b-buying-will-rewrite-the-rules-o.

5   Andy Hoar, "Death of a (B2B) Salesman," Forrester Research, last modified April 13, 2015, https://silo.tips/download/res122288.

6   Cespedes, chap. 11.

7   Phil Nanus and Stephen Fulkerson, "The State of The Customer Success 2021, Technology Services and Industry Association," Research Report, Technology and Services Industry Association, last modified February 2021, https://www.tsia.com/resources/the-state-of-customer-success-2021.

Chapter 23

1   B. H. Liddell Hart, *Strategy* (Hawthorne, CA: BN Publishing, 2020), Preface, location 49, Kindle.

2   Jerry Seinfeld, *Is This Anything?* (New York: Simon & Schuster, 2020), Kindle.

3   Dave Itzkoff, "Jerry Seinfeld Is Making Peace With Nothing: He's 'Post-Show Business,'" *New York Times*, May 4, 2020, https://www.nytimes.com/2020/05/04/arts/television/jerry-seinfeld-netflix.html.

4   Seinfeld, 5.

5   Read an excellent interview here: Tim Ferriss, "Jerry Seinfeld—A Comedy Legend's Systems, Routines, and Methods for Success," December 9, 2020, in *The Tim Ferriss Show*, podcast, https://tim.blog/2020/12/09/jerry-seinfeld-transcript/.

6   Daniel McGinn, "Life's Work: An Interview with Jerry Seinfeld," *Harvard Business Review*, January–February 2017, https://hbr.org/2017/01/lifes-work-jerry-seinfeld.

BIBLIOGRAPHY

Anderson, Chris. *The Long Tail: Why the Future of Business Is Selling Less of More*. Hachette Books, 2006. Kindle.

Ariely, Daniel. Predictably *Irrational: The Hidden Forces That Shape Our Decisions*. New York: HarperCollins, 2009. Kindle.

Berger, Jonah. *The Catalyst: How to Change Anyone's Mind*. New York: Simon & Schuster, 2020. Kindle.

Brafman, Ori, and Rom Brafman. *Sway: The Irresistible Pull of Irrational Behavior*. New York: Random House, 2009. Kindle.

Burkeman, Oliver. *Four Thousand Weeks: Time Management for Mortals*. New York: Farrar, Straus and Giroux, 2021. Kindle.

Cespedes, Frank V. *Aligning Strategy and Sales: The Choices, Systems, and Behaviors that Drive Effective Selling*. Boston: Harvard Business Review Press, 2014. Kindle.

Cespedes, Frank, and David Hoffeld. "Reframing Value in a Crisis." *Top Sales Magazine*, July 2020.

Cespedes, Frank V. *Sales Management That Works: How to Sell in a World That Never Stops Changing*. Boston: Harvard Business Review Press, 2021.

Cialdini, Robert. *Influence: The Psychology of Persuasion*. New York: HarperBusiness, 2021. Kindle.

Cialdini, Robert. *Pre-suasion: A Revolutionary Way to Influence and Persuade*. New York: Simon & Schuster, 2018. Kindle.

Clear, James. "Identity-Based Habits: How to Actually Stick to Your Goals This Year." Accessed February 15, 2022. https://jamesclear.com/identity-based-habits.

Covey, Stephen R. *The 7 Habits of Highly Effective People*. New York: Simon & Schuster, 1989. Kindle.

CSO Insights. "Running up the Down Escalator, 2017 CSO Insights World-Class Sales Practices Report." Accessed March 5, 2022. https://pleinairestrategies.com/wp-content/uploads/2017/12/2017-World-Class-Sales-Practices-Summary-Report.pdf

Doerr, John. *Measure What Matters: How Google, Bono, and the Gates Foundation Rock the World with OKRs*. New York: Penguin Random House, 2018. Kindle.

Drucker, Peter F. *The Essential Drucker: The Best of Sixty Years of Peter Drucker's Essential Writings on Management*. New York: HarperCollins, 2009. Kindle.

Drucker, Peter F. *The Practice of Management*. New York: HarperBusiness, 2014. Kindle.

Ferriss, Tim. "Jerry Seinfeld—A Comedy Legend's Systems, Routines, and Methods for Success (#485)." *The Tim Ferriss Show* (podcast). Last modified December 9, 2020. https://tim.blog/2020/12/09/jerry-seinfeld-transcript/

Freeman, Sir Lawrence. *Strategy: A History*. New York: Oxford University Press, 2013. Kindle.

Frei, Frances X., and Anne Morriss. "Begin with Trust." *Harvard Business Review* 98, no. 3 (2020): 112–121. https://hbr.org/2020/05/begin-with-trust.

Gartner. "5 Ways the Future of B2B Buying Will Rewrite the Rules of Effective Selling." August 4, 2020. https://www.gartner.com/en/documents/3988440/5-ways-the-future-of-b2b-buying-will-rewrite-the-rules-o.

Goffman, Irving. *The Presentation of the Self in Everyday Life*. New York: Anchor Books, 1959. Kindle.

Grenny, Joseph, David Maxfield, and Andrew Shimberg. "How to Have Influence." *MIT Sloan Management Review* 50, no. 1 (Fall 2008): 47. https://sloanreview.mit.edu/article/how-to-have-influence/.

Greeny, Joseph, Kerry Patterson, David Maxfield, Ron McMillan, and Al Switzler. *Influencer: The New Science of Leading Change*. New York: McGraw-Hill, 2013. Kindle.

Haidt, Jonathan. *The Happiness Hypothesis: Finding Modern Truth in Ancient Wisdom*. New York: Basic Books, 2006. Kindle.

Hart, B. H. Liddell. *Strategy*. Hawthorne, CA: BN Publishing, 2017. Kindle.

Heath, Chip, and Dan Heath. *Switch: How to Change When Things Are Hard*. New York: Currency Press, 2010. Kindle.

Hoar, Andy. "Death of a (B2B) Salesman." Forrester Research. Last modified April 13, 2015. https://silo.tips/download/res122288.

Hoffman, Reid. "Handcrafted: Brian Chesky, Co-founder & CEO of Airbnb." *Masters of Scale* podcast. https://mastersofscale.com/brian-chesky-handcrafted/.

Isaacson, Walter. *Steve Jobs*. New York: Simon & Schuster, 2011. Kindle.

Itzkoff, David. "Jerry Seinfeld Is Making Peace With Nothing: He's 'Post-Show Business'." *New York Times*, May 4, 2020. https://www.nytimes.com/2020/05/04/arts/television/jerry-seinfeld-netflix.html.

Kahneman, Daniel. *Thinking, Fast and Slow*. New York: Farrar, Straus and Giroux, 2011. Kindle.

Kahneman, Daniel, Jack L. Knetsch, and Richard H. Thaler. "Anomalies: The Endowment Effect, Loss Aversion, and Status Quo Bias." *The Journal of Economic Perspectives* 5(1) (Winter 1991): 193–206.

Kahneman, Daniel, Olivier Sibony, and Cass R. Sunstein. *Noise: A Flaw in Human Judgment*. New York: Little, Brown & Company, 2021. Kindle.

Kelly, Kevin. *The Inevitable: Understanding The 12 Technological Forces That Will Shape Our Future*. New York: Penguin, 2016. Kindle.

Koch, Richard. *The 80/20 Principle: The Secret to Achieving More with Less*. New York: Doubleday, 1998. Kindle.

Koch, Richard, and Greg Lockwood. *Superconnect: Harnessing the Power of Networks and the Strength of Weak Links*. New York: W. W. Norton, 2010. Kindle.

Kotter, John. *Leading Change*. Boston: Harvard Business Review Press, 2012. Kindle.

Kotter, John, and Dan S. Cohen. *The Heart of Change*. Boston: Harvard Business Review Press, 2012. Kindle.

Lakoff, George, and Mark Johnson. *Metaphors We Live By*. Chicago: University of Chicago Press, 1980. Kindle.

Laloux, Frédéric. *Reinventing Organizations: A Guide to Creating Organizations Inspired by the Next Stage in Human Consciousness.* Brussels, Belgium: Nelson Parker, 2014. Kindle.

Lehrer, Jonah. *How We Decide.* New York: Houghton Mifflin Harcourt, 2009. Kindle.

Lovallo, Dan, Tim Koller, Robert Uhlaner, and Daniel Kahneman. "Your Company Is Too Risk-Averse." *Harvard Business Review* 98, no. 2 (March–April, 2020): 104–111. https://hbr.org/2020/03/your-company-is-too-risk-averse.

Luntz, Frank. *Words That Work: It's Not What You Say, It's What People Hear.* New York: Hyperion, 2007. Kindle.

Maister, David H., Charles H. Green, and Robert M. Galford. *The Trusted Advisor.* New York: Simon & Shuster, 2000. Kindle.

Martin, Roger, and A. J. Lafley. *Playing to Win: How Strategy Really Works.* Boston: Harvard Business Review Press, 2013. Kindle.

McGinn, Daniel. "Life's Work: An Interview with Jerry Seinfeld." *Harvard Business Review,* January–February 2017. https://hbr.org/2017/01/lifes-work-jerry-seinfeld.

Mercier, Hugo. *The Enigma of Reason.* Boston: Harvard University Press, 2017. Kindle.

Moore, Geoffrey A. *Crossing the Chasm: Marketing and Selling Disruptive Products to Mainstream Customers.* Boston: Harper Business, 2014. Kindle.

Nanus, Phil, and Stephen Fulkerson. "The State of The Customer Success 2021, Technology Services and Industry Association." Research Report, Technology and Services Industry Association. Last modified February 2021. https://www.tsia.com/resources/the-state-of-customer-success-2021.

Pascale, Richard. *The Power of Positive Deviance: How Unlikely Innovators Solve the World's Toughest Problems*. Boston: Harvard Business Review Press, 2010. Kindle.

Pink, Daniel H. *To Sell Is Human: The Surprising Truth About Moving Others*. New York: Riverhead Books, 2012. Kindle.

Pollard, Timothy. *The Compelling Communicator: Mastering the Art and Science of Exceptional Presentation Design*. Washington, DC: Condor House Press, 2016. Kindle.

Pontefact, Dan. *Flat Army: Creating a Connected and Engaged Organization*. Hoboken, NJ: John Wiley & Sons, 2013. Kindle.

Raynor, Michael. *The Strategy Paradox*. New York, Doubleday, 2007. Kindle.

Redelmeier, D. A., J. Katz, and D. Kahneman. "Memories of Colonoscopy: A Randomized Trial." *Pain* 104, nos. 1–2 (2003 Jul): 187–94. doi: 10.1016/s0304-3959(03)00003-4. PMID: 12855328.

Ross, Lee, and Richard E. Nisbett. *The Person and the Situation: Perspectives of Social Psychology*. London: Pinter & Martin, 2011. Kindle.

Rumelt, Richard. *Good Strategy, Bad Strategy: The Difference and Why it Matters*. New York: Currency Press, 2011. Kindle.

Seinfeld, Jerry. *Is This Anything?* New York: Simon & Schuster, 2020. Kindle.

Simons, Robert. "Stress-Test Your Strategy: The 7 Questions to Ask." *Harvard Business Review* (2010): 92. https://hbr.org/2010/11/stress-test-your-strategy-the-7-questions-to-ask.

Stone, Brad. *The Everything Store: Jeff Bezos and the Age of Amazon*. New York: Little Brown & Co., 2013. Kindle.

Strohmetz, David B., Bruce Rind, Reed Fisher, and Michael Lynn. "Sweetening the Till: The Use of Candy to Increase

Restaurant Tipping." *Journal of Applied Social Psychology* 32 (2002): 300–309. https://files.secure.website/wscfus/5261551/uploads/Candy_Manuscript.pdf.

Sutherland, Rory. *Alchemy: The Dark Art and Curious Science of Creating Magic in Brands*, Business, and Life. London: HarperCollins, 2019. Kindle.

Sutherland, Rory. "The Objectivity Trap: On the Biases and Misconceptions That Cause Us All to Undervalue B2B Marketing." The B2B Institute of LinkedIn. Last modified July 2020. https://www.ogilvy.com/ideas/objectivity-trap.

Thaler, Richard H. *Misbehaving: The Making of Behavioral Economics*. New York: W. W. Norton, 2015. Kindle.

Thaler, Richard H., and Cass R. Sunstein. *Nudge: Improving Decisions About Health, Wealth, and Happiness*. New York: Penguin Books, 2008. Kindle.

Thomas, Janice, Connie L. Delisle, Kam Jugdev, and Pamela Buckle. "Selling Project Management to Senior Executives." Project Management Institute. Last modified June 24, 2000. https://www.pmi.org/learning/library/selling-project-management-senior-executives-143.

Toman, Nicholas, Brent Adamson, and Cristina Gomez. "The New Sales Imperative." *Harvard Business Review*, March–April 2017. https://hbr.org/2017/03/the-new-sales-imperative.

Urban, Tim. "The Cook and the Chef: Musk's Secret Sauce." *Wait But Why* (blog). November 6, 2015, https://waitbutwhy.com/2015/11/the-cook-and-the-chef-musks-secret-sauce.html.

Wilson, Timothy D. *Strangers to Ourselves: Discovering the Adaptive Unconscious*. Boston: Harvard University Press, 2004. Kindle.

INDEX

ABOUT THE AUTHOR

Douglas Cole is a sales leader at LinkedIn, an advisor with start-up accelerators in Canada and the United States, and a part-time university lecturer at The Rotman School of Management and The Schulich Executive Education Centre in Toronto. Over more than 20 years in consulting and sales, he has sold tens of millions of dollars in software-as-a-service and advisory work. He holds an MBA from The Wharton School, a Master's degree in International Studies from The Lauder Institute at the University of Pennsylvania, a Master's degree in English Literature from the University of Toronto, and a Bachelor's degree in Political Science and English Literature from the University of Toronto. He lives in Toronto, Canada, with his wife and two daughters.

Please find additional information at: **thesalesmba.ca** or **douglascole.ca**